HOTSPOTS
CORSICA

Written by Jane Anson
Original photography by Jacqueline Fryd
Front cover photography by Chris Lisle/CORBIS
Series design based on an original concept by Studio 183 Limited

Produced by Cambridge Publishing Management Limited
Project Editor: Rosalind Munro
Layout: Natalie White
Maps: PC Graphics

Published by Thomas Cook Publishing
A division of Thomas Cook Tour Operations Limited
Company Registration No. 1450464 England
PO Box 227, Unit 18, Coningsby Road
Peterborough PE3 8SB, United Kingdom
email: books@thomascook.com
www.thomascookpublishing.com
+ 44 (0) 1733 416477

ISBN: 978-1-84157-759-3

First edition © 2007 Thomas Cook Publishing
Text © 2007 Thomas Cook Publishing
Maps © 2007 Thomas Cook Publishing
Project Editor: Diane Ashmore
Production/DTP: Steven Collins

Printed and bound in Spain by GraphyCems

CONTENTS

WHAT'S IN YOUR GUIDEBOOK?

Independent authors Impartial up-to-date information from our travel experts who meticulously source local knowledge.

Experience Thomas Cook's 165 years in the travel industry and guidebook publishing enriches every word with expertise you can trust.

Travel know-how Contributions by thousands of staff around the globe, each one living and breathing travel.

Editors Travel-publishing professionals, pulling everything together to craft a perfect blend of words, pictures, maps and design.

You, the traveller We deliver a practical, no-nonsense approach to information, geared to how you really use it.

● *The beautiful Plage du Corsaire, Propriano*

INTRODUCTION
Getting to know Corsica

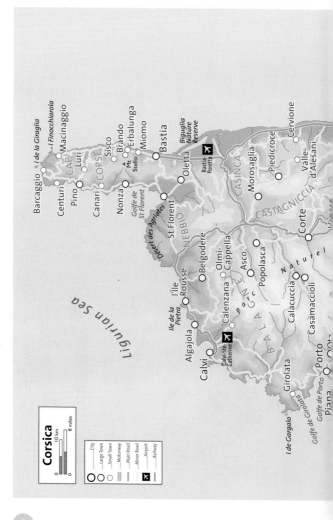

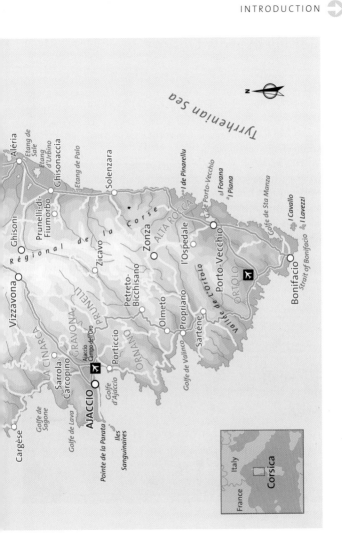

Getting to know Corsica

Anywhere that the ancient Greeks called 'Kallisté' (Most Beautiful) and that the French still call 'L'Île de Beauté' (The Beautiful Island) has got to have something going for it. You will start to see why it earned these sobriquets within a few minutes of landing: Corsica offers part Saint-Tropez, part the Hamptons, part Amalfi Coast, with a hefty dose of the Scottish highlands thrown in.

If the dramatically craggy landscape doesn't get you, the crystal-clear water and the endless shades of blue just might. A beautiful, unspoilt Mediterranean island, found almost halfway between France's Côte d'Azur and Italy's western coast, Corsica is easily accessible from both (it's actually a bit closer to Italy, making day trips there one of the added bonuses of your holiday). And it's sunnier than anywhere on mainland France!

● *Piedicroce, set high among chestnut trees*

The west coast and both 'tips' are the most beautiful – the east coast has a fairly large road running alongside it, but does have some wide sandy beaches, and a number of interesting places to explore. The west coast is more spectacular, but rockier and really fun to get to know by boat. Inland, the maquis, a dense carpet of scrub and forest, covers the island. And don't expect to get round Corsica in a day, even a few days. It's a large island, almost 9,000 sq km (3,475 sq miles), and the steep mountains inland (its highest peak being Monte Cinto at 2,710 m/8,891 ft) and winding cliff roads make exploring slow going at times – not least because you keep stopping the car to take photographs.

Once you've stopped gazing out to sea or up at the rocky cliffs and mountainous interior, you start to take in the atmosphere of the island, and its people. There's a multicultural feel – Corsica has been no stranger to invasions – part French, part Italian, part purely Corsican, meaning the food's good, the pace of life slow and the welcome genuine, particularly if you have warm words to offer about the island.

Its chequered history as a buffer zone for spats between France and Italy has marked out the island at every turn. It has actually been part of France for less than 250 years, after being sold by Genoa to Paris in 1768. Before that, this island belonged by turns to the Greeks, Romans, Vandals, Byzantines, Moors and Lombards. You're forever stumbling across crumbling citadels, watchtowers, ancient fortifications and monuments to those lost in battle. But there are also plenty of lively resorts, great scuba diving and surfing spots – and you can even ski in winter. The island's full-time population is just 260,000, but this swells to over two million in July and August, when the roads get even hairier than usual.

And of course one essential thing to know about Corsica is that its most famous son is Napoleon Bonaparte. Even if you didn't know this before arrival, you're unlikely to forget about him during your visit, particularly in the capital Ajaccio, where he was born. In fact, a good way to orientate yourself is by finding Café Bonaparte, or Rue Bonaparte, because you can pretty much guarantee there'll be one in every town.

THE BEST OF CORSICA

There are two speeds in Corsica, and they really depend on altitude. Inland, you'll be active – hiking, kayaking, abseiling, skiing – whereas on the coast, you'll be relaxed and laid back: whether on the beach, chilling out with cappuccinos in the many cafés, lazing on boat trips, or floating underwater admiring the coral and iridescent fish.

TOP 10 ATTRACTIONS

- **Saint-Florent** Often called Corsica's Saint-Tropez, go here for people-watching, yacht-envy, dining out and exploring the very pretty Old Town, with its citadel (see page 88).

- **L'Île Rousse** It's a (relatively) big town, but it is lively and has good nightlife, with films on at the open-air cinema every night in summer. Take a scuba diving course here, too (see page 32).

- **Calvi** A good marina, full of lively eating places and boats speeding off to Scandola and Girolata, makes Calvi one of the best spots on the island. And every June there's the Jazz Festival (see page 27).

- **Girolata** This tiny village on the Gulf of Porto is only connected to the rest of the gulf by a mule track, and has practically no electricity or telephones. Famous for its seafood restaurants, it's the ultimate getaway (see page 80).

- **Bonifacio** Probably the most beautiful town on the island, Bonifacio is surrounded by fortifications and perched giddily on cliffs above the sea. Take boat trips around the caves (see page 55).

- **Porto-Vecchio** This is the place to party: a big Italian tourist resort, which means you start eating and partying later here than in 'French-style' resorts (see page 51).

- **Propriano** There is still good coral around the coast, although it's getting rarer all the time: you can scuba-dive and snorkel here to your heart's content. It is an attractive port with lovely beaches nearby (see page 60).

- **Cap Corse** A gorgeous part of the island with amazing beaches and mountain villages. Many of Corsica's best wine growers are based here (see page 36).

- **Corte** A pretty old town in the mountains, it's the point of departure for walks, mountain biking, horse riding, abseiling... and skiing in winter (see page 47).

- **Les Calanques** Just two hair-raising kilometres ($1^1/_4$ miles) off the D81 road near Porto, but with gorgeous rocky scenery and straight drops down to the sea (see page 79).

🔽 *Ajaccio's famous lion fountain*

SYMBOLS KEY

The following symbols are used throughout this book:

ⓐ address **ⓣ** telephone **ⓕ** fax **ⓔ** email **ⓦ** website address
ⓛ opening times **Ⓝ** public transport connections **ⓘ** important

---

The following symbols are used on the maps:

ⓘ information office	**O**	city
✉ post office	**O**	large town
▣ shopping	○	small town
✈ airport	**▪**	poi (point of interest)
✚ hospital	**═══**	motorway
▨ police station	**———**	main road
▤ bus station	**———**	minor road
▧ railway station	**—**	railway
✝ church		

❶ numbers denote featured cafés, restaurants & evening venues

RESTAURANT CATEGORIES

The symbol after the name of each restaurant listed in this guide indicates the price of a typical three-course meal without drinks for one person:

£ under €15   **££** €15–€30   **£££** over €30

⊙ *Porto's tower was built by the Genoese in 1549*

RESORTS
Places under the sun

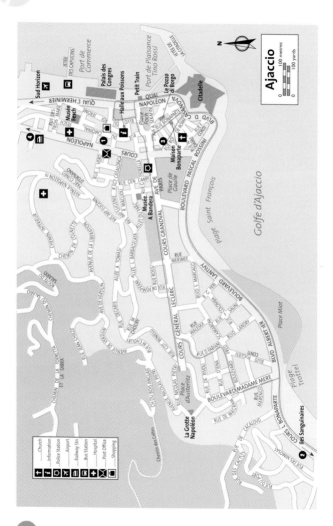

Ajaccio

0 ___ 100 metres
0 ___ 100 yards

Church
Information
Police Station
Airport
Railway Stn
Bus Station
Hospital
Post Office
Shopping

Ajaccio

The capital city, and site of the island's main airport, Ajaccio deserves far more than a cursory glance. On an island with this much natural beauty, it's easy to drive through the built-up areas and head straight for the beach – but there's so much to enjoy about the capital, so take a few days to get to know it. If you arrive by boat, you'll land at the Jetée des Capucins, but the best harbour from which to watch the world go by is Tino Rossi by the Citadel.

There are apartment blocks, and uglier outskirts, as with any capital city, but head to the Old Town (which means everything from Place du Général de Gaulle to the west, the Citadel to the southeast and Place du Maréchal Foch to the north, with its lion-guarded fountain like a tiny Trafalgar Square) and you'll be charmed by the architecture and the palm-lined squares. You'll learn far more about how the island works by spending a morning watching the locals haggle at the César-Campinchi market, or the fishermen unload their catches at the port, than you will from days driving a hire car around the island's roads – and if that's not enough, the names of the roads, the monuments and the museums give you a crash course in its history. The town of Porticcio is very close to Ajaccio (it's basically an extension of the city, like a highly glamorous suburb), and is the place to go for many of the restaurants and nightclubs, although they've managed to squeeze quite a lot of good nightlife into the downtown area as well.

Ajaccio is an elegant town, despite the crowds, and has the ever-present backdrop of the mountains (which are usually snow-capped right up until April). The people are really friendly, and love to hear how well placed their city is, right in the cradle of this beautiful gulf. As you will quickly learn, this is Napoleon's birthplace too, so get ready for postcards, tea towels, cafés, statues and even buses all bearing his image!

BEACHES

There are not many beaches right near the centre (with the exception of the Plage de Saint-François), but there are more than enough superb stretches of sand within easy reach along the Gulf of Ajaccio: Marinella beach to the north, Parata Point and the beaches of the Capo di Feno. There's also a good port in the city itself, if you get a hankering for boats and water. Corsica's biggest water park, Acqua Cyrne Gliss, is in Porticcio.

Acqua Cyrne Gliss

ⓐ Route Départementale 55, Porticcio ⓣ 04 95 25 17 48 ⓕ 04 95 25 04 48 ⓔ info@acquagliss.com ⓦ www.acquagliss.com ⓛ 10.30–19.00 July & Aug; 11.00–18.00 May, June & Sept; closed Oct–Mar ❶ Admission charge

Capo di Feno

An exposed reef that is good for surfing as you get good breakers, particularly in spring and autumn, but you need to know what you're doing and it is definitely not for beginners. There's a small but pretty

⬤ Looking towards Ajaccio from the south

beach but no cafés or restaurants. It is accessed by a small path leading from Pointe de la Parata (Parata Point). It is also worth knowing that from the Tour de la Parata, built in 1608 to defend the coast from pirates, the view of the gulf is absolutely spectacular. No buses

Marinella Beach
Plenty of white sand and a tree-lined backdrop make this a very popular spot with the locals at weekends, not just in summer. This beach featured in the crooning ballads of 1930s singer-turned-actor Tino Rossi, possibly Ajaccio's most famous son after Napoleon (and yes, that's him again in the name of Ajaccio's Port de Plaisance).
Bus No 5

Plage de Ricanto (Ricanto Beach)
Between Ajaccio and Porticcio, this is an urban beach (as far as Corsica gets) and can at times be a bit dirty, with city debris such as cans and wrappers knocking about, but they have been having some major cleaning-up sessions recently, and the beach is being restored to its sparkling best. Bus No 8

THINGS TO SEE & DO

The port is great fun all day long: from early morning when fishermen bring in their catches to throwing-out time when late-night revellers are forced to head for home. The Old Town, too, is good for strolling around – it has a Citadel (not open to the public, but it still looks good for an evening stroll), the gorgeous Place du Maréchal Foch, and a large cathedral (where Napoleon was christened in 1771). And talking of Napoleon, Ajaccio is Bonaparte heaven – monuments, museums and souvenir shops are all full of artefacts relating to his life and famous victories (with perhaps a judicious brushing over of how he ended up).

The modern section of the town is obviously less picturesque, but contains some good shops and galleries; Ajaccio is very big on its art, particularly Italian – in fact there are many parts of this island where you get the feeling they might well have been supporting the Italians rather than the French in the 2006 World Cup final. Every June, there's a big procession in honour of Saint Erasme, patron saint of fishermen.

Ajaccio is also a good shopping town, where you can stock up on clothes and sun gear, and get seriously kitted up for some watersport action. The main shopping street is called – wait for it – cours Napoléon.

There are buses around town, but not many. From the train station, go up the steps and turn right and you'll see the bus stops. Numbers 3 and 4 go down into the main part of town.

Halle aux Poissons (Fish Market)
Strictly for fish lovers, this is the daily professional fish market where visitors are allowed to watch. Be careful: the floors are very slippery.
ⓐ Place du Marché ⓛ 07.00–13.00 & 17.00–19.00 Tues–Sun

Maison Bonaparte
Birthplace of Napoleon. There is also a Napoleon Museum at the Hotel de Ville in Place Foch, but this one is smaller and more intimate.
ⓐ Rue Saint Charles ⓣ 04 95 21 43 89 ⓕ 04 95 21 61 32 ⓛ 09.00–13.00 & 14.00–18.00 (summer); 10.00–11.30 & 14.00–16.15 (winter)
ⓔ maison.bonaparte@culture.gouv.fr

Musée A Bandera (Bandera Museum)
Small but interesting museum, looking at Corsican and Mediterranean history up to World War II.
ⓐ 1 rue du Général Levie ⓣ 04 95 51 07 34 ⓕ 04 95 51 39 60 ⓛ 09.00–19.00 Mon–Fri, Apr–Oct; 09.00–12.00 & 14.00–18.00 Mon–Fri, Nov–Mar

Musée Fesch
This museum houses an extremely important collection of Italian art put together by Cardinal Fesch, Napoleon's uncle. It houses works by key artists from Botticelli, via Poussin to Canova. Good English labelling.
ⓐ 50–52 rue Cardinal Fesch ⓣ 04 95 21 48 17 ⓕ 04 95 21 80 94
ⓔ musee.fesch@ville-ajaccio.fr ⓦ www.musee-fesch.com

ALL YOU EVER NEEDED TO KNOW ABOUT NAPOLEON...

- Born in Ajaccio in 1769 and died on St Helena in 1821, Napoleon was known as 'The Little Corporal', even though he wasn't all that short for an 18th-century Frenchman – he was 1.68 m (5 ft 6 in) tall.
- He became France's first consul in 1799, then first consul for life in 1802, and finally emperor from 1804 until 1815.
- After taking France on a decade-long battle-winning streak, he eventually abdicated after leading his army into Russia and losing 80 per cent of his troops, his final defeat being at Waterloo in 1815.
- Oh, and one other famous defeat was by Nelson at the Battle of Trafalgar in 1805.
- He was married first to Josephine de Beauharnais from 1796 until 1809, and then to Marie-Louise of Austria from 1810 until his death.
- Josephine agreed to divorce him to allow him to marry again and produce an heir, but their own letters show that they remained very much in love.
- Napoleon was briefly exiled to the island of Elba, but managed to get back to France. He became emperor again for 100 days, after which he was promptly stripped of all titles and sent for his final exile to St Helena.
- Although there are rumours that he died of arsenic poisoning, it is more likely that he had stomach cancer.
- The current French civil laws are still based on the Napoleonic Code that he drew up in the early 19th century.
- One anecdote about Napoleon tells how, after his ill-fated invasion of Russia in 1812, he became very worried by reports of trouble back in France. Leaving his army, he headed back to his homeland. When he arrived at the River Neman, he asked the Russian ferryman if many deserters had passed that way. 'No,' the man replied, 'you are the first.'

🕙 09.30–12.00 & 14.00–18.00 Tues–Sun, 1 Apr–30 June; 14.00–18.00 Mon, 09.30–18.00 Tues–Thur, 10.30–18.00 Sat & Sun, July & Aug; 09.30–12.00 & 14.00–18.00 Tues–Sun, Sept; 09.30–12.00 & 14.00–18.00 Tues–Fri & Sun, Oct–Mar ❶ Admission charge

Petit Train des Îles

A tourist train that winds up along the coast, this is ideal if you've got little ones in tow who get tired easily. You can choose between two circuits – one around the Old Town and the other heading out towards the Îles Sanguinaires, ending up at the Pointe de la Parata. Both allow you to get out and explore at certain key points.

ⓐ 2 quai Napoléon, Ajaccio ❶ 04 95 51 13 69 🆆 www.petit-train-ajaccio.com ❶ Admission charge

Le Pozzo di Borgo

Opening in late 2007, this is the long-awaited renovation of one of Ajaccio's most historic buildings and the family house of Count Charles-André Pozzo di Borgo, who was first friend, then sworn enemy, of Napoleon (which might be why the house has been left in ruins for so long). It is presently being converted into a luxury hotel; when it opens, be sure to check out the *trompe l'oeil* effect of its front walls, and linger over a cocktail at the bar. The outside is well worth a look, too.

ⓐ Rue Bonaparte

Sud Horizon

This is the place to hire wetsuits, flippers, snorkels, even small boats.

ⓐ Route de Alata, La Louisiane ❶ 04 95 23 48 07 🆆 www.sudhorizon.net 🕙 09.00–12.00 & 14.00–18.00 Mon–Sat (summer); Mon–Fri (winter)

TAKING A BREAK

Bars & cafés

There are a good array of both in Ajaccio – but, wherever you end up, you have to try the local sardines (either *farci*, which means stuffed;

⬥ *A fisherman mends his nets in Ajaccio harbour*

escabeche, which means served cold with mint and vinegar; Sicilian style with tomato sauce; *beignet* (battered and fried) or just simply grilled with lemon).

Le Grand Café Napoléon £ ❶ Expect to find a café with this name in every town in Corsica, but this is a good one to get started with. It is housed in one of the oldest buildings in Ajaccio. There is a huge terrace for coffees and drinks outside; be warned that food can start to get pricey inside. There is also a restaurant, which is mid-range in price.
ⓐ 10 cours Napoléon ① 04 95 21 42 54 ① 04 95 21 53 32
⊙ 07.00–23.00 Mon–Fri, 08.00–20.00 Sat; closed late evening Sat & all day Sun

AFTER DARK

Restaurants
Coté Plage £ ❷ Very chilled, laid-back place, with good views. Food here is international style with a heavy emphasis on seafood. ⓐ Route des Sanguinaires, Plage de Barbicaja ① 04 95 52 07 78 ⊙ 10.00–22.00, summer; 11.00–15.00 & 19.00–21.00, winter

L'Estaminet ££ ❸ You're very definitely in French rather than Italian Corsica here. This provides a full-on Gallic menu, and a great wine list. One of the real finds in Ajaccio. ⓐ 6 rue du Roi de Rome ① 04 95 50 10 42
⊙ 12.00–14.00 & 19.00–20.00 Mon–Sat

Clubs
Blue Moon ££ ❹ Nightclub in Porticcio, just outside the main centre of Ajaccio. ⓐ Residence Les Marines, Porticcio ① 04 95 25 07 70
⊙ 24.00–04.00 Ⓝ Bus from Ajaccio to Porticcio
❶ Admission charge

Porto

A small resort in the south of the island, halfway between Calvi and Ajaccio, Porto's dramatic bay opens onto the Gulf of Porto, a UNESCO World Heritage Site, which gives you some idea of its scale and impact. And pretty much as soon as the beach stops, the mountains seem to take off. Porto is built around a huge forest of eucalyptus trees, which give a gorgeous scent to the air. One of the most famous sights is the Genoese Tower that stands over the harbour, and there are plenty of other reminders of the Genoese reign in the roads and mountains around the town. From here as well you have the Calanques, Girolata and Scandola nature reserves, all within easy reach.

BEACHES

There is a pretty (but with large pebbles, rather than white sand) beach in Porto itself, and plenty of coastline on either side. There's even a Route des Plages, which sounds fairly promising, extending about 40 km (25 miles) out from Porto to the La Croix Pass.

Plage d'Arone
About 11 km (7 miles) from Piana in the Gulf of Porto, and one of the loveliest beaches. You get to this from the Corniche road.

Plage du Bussaglia
This has big pudding stones. It is a good place for hiring canoes.

THINGS TO SEE & DO

There's the popular Aquarium de la Poudrière. This is where you take the gorgeous drive along the Calanques and into the Scandola Nature Reserve. The tiny village of Girolata is also within easy distance of Porto (see page 80).

◆ *The steep hills slope down to the turquoise sea at Porto*

Aquarium de la Poudrière

This is not too big, but they've certainly made the most of the space; it's full to the brim with oceanographic, biological and gastronomic information on fish – and there are a few big examples swimming around as well. The labelling is in French.

🅐 Porto la Marine 🕓 04 95 26 19 24 🅕 04 95 26 19 23
🅔 aquariumporto@m6net.fr 🕒 09.00–22.00 daily, July & August; 09.00–19.00 May, June & Sept; 09.00–12.00 & 13.00–17.00 over winter (sometimes 10.00–17.00 during winter: check ahead)
🅘 Admission charge

TAKING A BREAK

Restaurants

Beau Séjour £ This hotel restaurant serves traditional Corsican food, including wild boar and fish. 🅐 Quartier Vaita 🕓 04 95 26 12 11
🕒 Open all year

Chez Marie £ About 5 km (3 miles) outside of Porto on the D124, this is a restaurant, bar and very friendly *chambre d'hôtes*. You don't need to stay here to sample their plentiful local specialities, from wild boar to the local soup. 🅐 Chez Marie/Bar des Chasseurs, Ota 🕓 04 95 26 11 37
🕒 Open all year, and it's worth trying your luck for some food at any time

La Mer ££ Practically dipping its feet in the water, this restaurant is easy to find, right at the end of the marina. It serves freshly caught, simply presented fish. 🅐 La Marine 🕓 04 95 26 11 27 🕒 12.00–14.00 & 19.00–23.30 July & Aug; 12.00–14.00 & 19.00–21.30 Mar–June & Sept–Oct; closed early Nov–mid-Mar

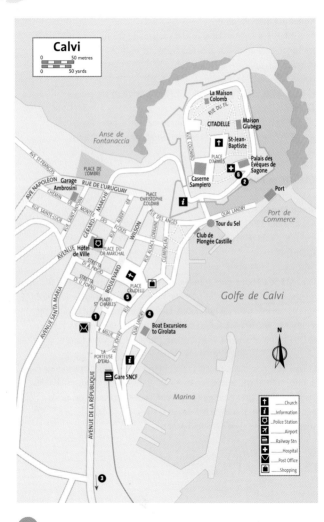

Calvi

0   50 metres
0   50 yards

Anse de
Fontanaccia

La Maison
Colomb

RUE DU FIL

CITADELLE

Maison
Giubega

RUE COLOMB

St-Jean-
Baptiste

PLACE
D'ARMES

Palais des
Evêques de
Sagone

6

Caserne
Sampiero

Port

AVE ST-FRANÇOIS

PLACE DE
L'OMBRE

AVE NAPOLÉON

Garage
Ambrosini

RUE DE L'URUGUAY

PLACE
CHRISTOPHE
COLOMB

2

CHEMIN DE

RUE SAINTE-LUCIE

RUE SAINT-ANTOINE

MONTÉE

GÉRARD

MARCHÉ

RUE ALBERT 1er

RUE DES ÉCOLES

RUE DES ANGES

i

QUAI LANDRY

Tour du Sel

Port de
Commerce

RUE EUSSE FORTUNE

CLEMENCEAU

Club de
Plongée Castille

AVENUE

Hôtel
de Ville

WILSON

PLACE DU
DR-MARCHAL

STRETTA
DI A. PROGDI

STRETTA
DI U. FORNU

BOULEVARD

PLACE
CRUDELLI

5

RUE

Golfe de Calvi

AVENUE SANTA MARIA

PLACE
ST-CHARLES

1

4

QUAI LANDRY

Boat Excursions
to Girolata

R. MILLIU

LA
PORTEUSE
D'EAU

RUE OPALE

i

AVENUE DE LA RÉPUBLIQUE

Gare SNCF

Marina

N

3

	Church
i	Information
	Police Station
✈	Airport
	Railway Stn
✚	Hospital
	Post Office
	Shopping

Calvi

Calvi is a lively tourist resort of the type that Corsica specialises in: it has a beautiful Citadel – which gets brilliantly lit up at night – sitting on a promontory overlooking the sparklingly blue sea, with a backdrop of some stunning mountains. It's one of the best underwater sites in Corsica as well, so if you like diving, you're going to be happy here. If you can arrive by boat, do so, because you will have a stunning view of this amazing Citadel rising up out of nowhere, brooding and forbidding, contrasting completely with the long sandy beach that stretches out from the town, and the gentle pine trees all around.

Forget Bonaparte here (well, all right, they might have squeezed in one avenue Napoléon, and it turns out he spent some time hiding out here with his family), but they have their own famous son. Christopher Columbus was supposedly born in Calvi in 1450, and there's a large, attractive square named after him in the centre – as well as a festival dedicated to him every October. And that's not all: this is also where Nelson lost the sight in one eye after battling the French, and then – quite reasonably – declared he never wanted to see the place again with his remaining eye.

Calvi is the closest spot to the French Provençal coast, and the capital of the 'Balagne', the inland hilly region of huddled, tile-roofed stone villages that is becoming known as the 'Luberon' of Corsica as it moves upmarket.

In terms of getting around, Calvi has the main RN197 connecting it to Ajaccio, and the local D81b that takes you (slowly but prettily) to Bastia. Buses are run by Les Beaux Voyages ⓐ Place de la Porteuse d'Eau ⓣ 04 95 65 15 02 ⓦ www.lesbeauxvoyagesencorse.com ⓝ Buses run daily except Sunday between Calvi, l'Île Rousse and Bastia; but note that getting inland will be more difficult as there are no regular bus routes

○ *Calvi's impressive Citadelle*

BEACHES

The area is full of long sandy beaches. The best one stretches for 5 km (3 miles), almost directly from the town itself.

Le Plage de Calvi

This beach, separated from the main town only by a small road, offers lovely views back over Calvi and the Citadel. The section that is closest to town is also best for swimming, as the beach shelves gently out to the sea. In July and August, the road back from this beach to Calvi can turn into one long, over-heated traffic jam. Far better to go to the beach early in the morning, head back after lunch for a siesta, then spend a few hours strolling around the pedestrianised roads in the Citadel in the afternoon.

You can also go on **donkey rides** from Sant'Antonino in the Balagne, just northeast of Calvi.

THINGS TO SEE & DO

In this, the second most popular tourist destination on the island, there is plenty to keep you occupied. In Calvi itself, there's another great Citadel, with winding silent streets and some excellent fortifications, but really you come to Calvi for the sea, the port, the lively restaurants and the fun atmosphere. And don't forget the **Jazz Festival** in June and **La Festival du Vent** (the Wind Festival) in October (see page 108).

Behind the quayside are steps leading up to the picturesque rue Clemenceau, a pedestrianised street thronging with people strolling by the shops and restaurants. If you can avoid the Christopher Columbus tea towels, and the replica Corsica flags, there are some good ice-cream shops, delis and a few interesting clothes boutiques.

From the port, you can take plenty of **boat trips** round the coast – try Colombo Line on ➌ Quai Landry ➊ 04 95 65 32 10 Ⓦ www.colombo-line.com

AOC Calvi's ten wine makers have established a **Wine Route** (*route des vins*) to encourage you to visit the vineyards: more details from ⓦ www.vinsdecorse.com

Citadelle
The Citadel represents six centuries of Genoese rule, and is one of the most interesting on the island. As at Bonifacio, the entrance is really amazing, with its thick stone archway; an art exhibition greets you on the other side. Inside, the streets are narrow, steep and cobbled: a pretty dangerous combination.
Ⓝ None, but the little tourist train runs up to the Citadel

Club de Plongée Castille
Just two minutes' walk from the station, right in the port, this is the oldest diving club in town. It is great for both beginners and experts.
ⓐ Port de Calvi ⓣ 04 95 65 14 05 ⓦ www.plongeecastille.com Ⓛ Dives at 08.30, 10.30, 14.30 & 16.30 (summer), by reservation; dives at 09.00, 11.00 & 15.00 (winter), by reservation

Église St Jean Baptiste
Approached by a crumbling set of stone steps, this attractive church is best viewed from the inside, on a sunny day, when sunlight streams in through the many tiny windows that ring the top of the building.
ⓐ Place des Armes

TAKING A BREAK

Bars & cafés
Boulangerie Galetti £ ❶   Very well located just behind Quai Landry, this has an excellent range of pastries, and a cheerful coffee shop next door that you can take them in to eat. ⓐ 4 boulevard Wilson
ⓣ and ⓕ 04 95 65 01 60 Ⓛ 06.30–19.00

AFTER DARK

Restaurants

You're not going to find it hard to eat well in Calvi – just head to the marina and follow the crowds.

A Candella £ ❷   Right in the Citadel, next to the oratory of Saint Antoine, this serves up well-priced local specialities. ⓐ Rue Saint Antoine ⓣ 04 95 65 42 13 ⓛ Apr–Sept

Calvi Fornia ££ ❸   Good bistro fare of *moules frites* and mixed grills. There is also live music every night – great fun. ⓐ Plage de la Pinède ⓣ 04 95 46 37 30 ⓛ 12.00–23.00 July & Aug; 12.00–02.00 & 18.00–23.00, Apr–Oct

Emile's ££ ❹   Lunch or dinner, right on the port, this place is great! ⓐ Quai Landry ⓣ 04 95 65 22 18 ⓦ www.restaurant-emiles.com ⓛ Daily in summer; Wed–Sun, Oct–Mar

Le Tire Bouchon ££ ❺   Excellent local specialities, including wines. It also has a terrace. ⓐ 15 rue Clemenceau ⓣ 04 95 65 25 41 ⓛ 12.00–14.00 & 19.30–23.00 Thur–Tues; closed Nov–Mar

Bars

Chez Tao ££ ❻   The coolest piano bar in town, if that isn't a contradiction in terms! This has a lively bar, and a terrace where you can watch the sun go down ... or come up. ⓐ La Citadelle ⓣ 04 95 65 00 73 ⓛ 20.00–late

L'Île Rousse

No, not some disputed Russian-owned islands just off the coast, but a fairly modern and attractive city around 28 km (18 miles) east of Calvi. The Italian version of the name is Isola Rossa (Red Island), and it is named for the deep russet-red colour that the buildings turn at sunset. There's a lively port, smartly paved streets and plenty of shops, so it's a good place in which to stock up if you need anything before heading inland. The main square is called Place Paoli, and is shaded with plane trees. The Old Town and the main shopping areas fan out from one side of this square (the other side opens out onto the sea), so it's always a good place to arrange to meet up. In the middle of the square, alongside the lovely fountain, Corsicans while away their summers playing *boules* (go on, by now you know you want to join them).

The local bus service is run by Les Supers ⓐ Boulevard de Fogata, Propriété Molinari ⓣ 04 95 60 01 56 ⓝ Transport Santini run a bus service between Bastia, Saint-Florent and L'Île Rousse (ⓣ (info) 04 95 37 02 98)

BEACHES

The main beach at Ile Rousse is in the centre of the town and, as at Calvi, it is accessible by train. The sand is fine and golden, the sea clear and blue and there are watersports and fishing trips from the beach. Some of the restaurants heading away from the town hire out sunloungers if you want to relax in comfort.

Alternatively, head out of the town for around 3 km (1¹/₄ miles) and you'll find (if you've been well directed – best to get a local to tell you) a dirt track that heads down to the **Plage de Rindara**.

Plage de Bodri
A little further along between Algajola and l'Île Rousse is Bodri Plage, a long stretch of sand with turquoise, clear waters. There's a car park about 500 m (550 yds) from the beach itself, but it's worth the walk – and right

next to it is Giunchetu Bay, where the beach shelves gently, making it perfect for children.

Plage de Lozari
Slightly further out of town, but the sand here is flatter and whiter. The beach is very relaxed and in the summer there are watersports and a little café. Access to the beach is via a road off the N197 between turnings for Palasca and Belgodère.

Plage de Rindara
Impressively sized sand dunes mark this beach, making it good for walks.

THINGS TO SEE & DO

The Old Town isn't really too old here, but it's still very pretty, with a covered market and plenty of pretty roads leading down to the sea. Obviously you need to linger and drink coffee in Place Paoli, and contemplate the fountain with its bust of 'U Babbu di u Patria' (Father of the Nation), one of many local tributes to Pascal Paoli. The Aquarium has recently closed, so you'll have to go scuba diving if you want to get live fish viewing.

Covered Market
Just by Place Paoli is a classically colonnaded building that hosts a market every morning. At weekends the emphasis is more on antiques, while on weekdays the stalls are concentrated on food.

École du Plongée de l'Île Rousse
ⓐ Route du Port ⓣ 04 95 60 22 55 ⓦ www.plongee-ilerousse.com

Île de la Pietra
Not really an island, because it's linked by a little jetty, but this is the red-rocked outcrop that gives the town its name. It makes a good evening stroll to see the lighthouse and the little tower, which now often holds painting exhibitions.

⬥ *The main square, Place Paoli, is full of cafés that offer some shade*

Lighthouse

The grounds of the lighthouse are open to the public, and there are great views back over the town.

Le Petit Tramway de Balagne

Another of those tourist trains that Corsica does so well, this runs once a day between l'Île Rousse and Calvi. Info at the stations at Calvi or l'Île Rousse ❶ 04 95 60 00 50 ❷ Apr–Oct

TAKING A BREAK

Bars & restaurants

Au Bon Vin Corse £ A wine bar and shop that also has a very nice terrace and looks out onto a quiet square. ❶ Place Delanney ❶ 04 95 60 15 14 ❷ 08.00–22.00 Mon–Sat, 08.00–12.00 Sun (summer); Wed, Sat & Sun (winter); closed Dec & Jan

AFTER DARK

Restaurants

Le Bistro de la Place ££ Newly opened. No menus, but well priced à la carte from around €30. The chef Cedrik Dullier is Belgian and uses plenty of locally sourced seasonal produce. When busy, or particularly sunny, the restaurant spills out onto the square. ❶ Place Paoli ❶ 04 95 60 12 90 ❷ Daily, June–Sept; Mon eve–Sat, Oct–May

La Bodega ££ Guitars and local singers make evenings here always fun. And to add to the sense of fun, the menu offers good sharing food like paella. ❶ 7 rue Napoléon ❶ 04 95 33 20 97. ❷ 20.00–late

Cap Corse

The northern tip of Corsica, and its sunniest part, Cap Corse, is 40 km (25 miles) in length, and perfect for hiking, cycling and all types of leisurely exploration. It has a narrow spine of mountains, which rise over 914 m (3,000 ft) above sea level, running down the middle. On the east side, a series of small villages cuddle into coves, while on the west coast the settlements are higher up on the cliffs, more directly exposed to pounding waves and heavy storms. Hikers head for the many walking trails, such as the well-known Sentier des Douaniers (at some points from here, you can see the sea on both sides). Make sure the camera is loaded for the panoramic viewpoints of Capo Grosso, Moulin Mattei and the Tour de Seneque, above Pino. The vineyards of Patrimonio are renowned, particularly for their Muscat, and most wineries welcome visitors for wine tasting. The wine route, or 'route des vins', is signposted from Saint-Florent.

BEACHES

Many of the beaches are shingle, but there are still lots of sunbathing opportunities. The best stretch of sandy beach is **Plage de Tamarone**, near Macinaggio, but also try **Barcaggio** and **Nonza**. Try taking the boat from Saint-Florent to the beach in the **Désert des Agriates**, opposite the big bay of Saint-Florent, where you can take spectacular photos.

THINGS TO SEE & DO

You're most definitely not going to be bored exploring Cap Corse (and don't forget that exploration by boat is positively encouraged!). There are plenty of sandy coves and fishing villages that you'll just stumble across, including Centuri-Port, Erbalunga and Macinaggio, and don't miss the villages perched up in the hillside like Rogliano, Cannelle and Nonza. The D238 out of Saint-Florent leads to the **Cathedral of the Nebbio**, a very old Romanesque church. It then carries on to a very dramatic area with lots of little villages – the region is also called the Nebbio.

A Cunfraternita

Wine museum in Luri, with opportunities to taste local wines.
ⓐ Marie de Luri, Luri ⓣ 04 95 35 06 44 ⓦ www.acunfraternita.com
ⓛ 10.00–12.00 & 15.00–18.00 July & Aug; rest of the year, phone ahead for times ⓘ Admission charge

Cava de Brando

Horse riding, from €14 for an hour's riding. They don't have any ponies, though, so it's not for little children.
ⓐ Glacier de Brando ⓣ 04 95 33 94 02

Centuri Port

This is the best place to stop for a picnic, and there's a lovely fishing port with little restaurants. You can go out on boat trips, too.

Costume Museum

This small museum displays around 50 costumes representative of the whole of Corsica from the past 200 years.
ⓐ St François Monastery, Canari, on the west coast of Cap Corse
ⓣ 04 95 37 80 53

La Côte Septentrionale

The wildest and most remote part of the coastland, where you can discover empty beaches even in high summer. The whole place only has two tiny villages, Tollare and Barcaggio. It is accessible from Centuri, or from Macinaggio port.

Dollfin Diving Club

Dives for beginners and experts.
ⓐ Marine de Sisco, Sisco ⓣ 04 95 58 26 16 ⓦ www.dollfin.fr

Erbalunga

Erbalunga is another chic fishing port on the western Cap, with a lively central square and lots of restaurants. In recent years, this has become more and more hip, so expect clothes boutiques and art galleries. Each August, a music festival takes place down by the harbour. This spot was very popular with painters in the 1930s; no less so today, one imagines, because this is classically inspiring stuff. Le Pirat on Erbalunga's waterfront is great for local specialities: seafood, liqueur-infused desserts and hand-made cheeses from the Cap Corse.

Luri

The commune of Luri goes from the mountain to the sea where there is a miniature harbour with a little beach, a few restaurants and a hotel by the beach. The Luri is actually the name of the river that runs through the area, with 17 tiny hamlets, some only a collection of a few houses. The island's biggest wine fair is held here every July.

Monte Stello

This mountain, at 1,300 m (4,265 ft) high, makes a good day-trip option from wherever you are based in Cap Corse.

Mountain and hill walks

You've really got to throw on a pair of walking boots at some point during your visit. There are hiking trails all over the Cap. Aside from Monte Stello (see above), some of the best walks start from Luri, Olcani and Olmeta di Capo Corso.

Nonza

This is one of the prettiest villages on the whole island. There's an 18th-century tower, the Sainte Julie Church and not much else. The beach has big black stones, which makes for a welcome change after all that gorgeous white sand!

La Tour de Sénèque

At the top of the Sainte Lucie pass (the road that links east and west sections of the Cap), the tower dominates the valley.

🔺 *Nonza sits high up on Cap Corse*

Wine growers

Particularly welcoming is Lina Pieretti-Venturi of Domaine Pieretti in Luri, a female grower (there's only one other in Corsica). With just 5 hectares (12¹/₂ acres) of vines, she makes a gorgeous 100 per cent Muscat à Petit Grains.

Domaine Pieretti Lina Pieretti-Venturi, Santa Severa, Luri
 and 04 95 35 01 03

TAKING A BREAK

Bars & restaurants

The whole place is full of great restaurants and undiscovered bars – but the pace is far slower than in Ajaccio or Porto-Vecchio, so expect nightlife to stop rather than start at midnight.

U Capezzu £ Unpretentious place with wooden tables and fresh fish.
 Santa Severa, Marine de Luire, Luri 04 95 35 03 23

Ferme Auberge de Campo di Monte £ Pull up a chair here and enjoy watching the staff bring you copious portions of whatever fish is in season. Murato 04 95 37 64 39

La Terrasse £ Cheerful, fast service at this popular eating spot.
 Erbalunga, Brando 04 95 33 96 28

Castel Brando ££ Lovely hotel where non-residents can also eat evening meals. Erbalunga 04 95 30 10 30 04 95 33 98 18
 info@castelbrando.com www.castelbrando.com

Osteria di u Porto ££ Charming restaurant opposite the port serving traditional seafood. Macinaggio 04 95 35 40 49

Bastia

Bastia is Corsica's northern capital. It also has an airport, but – unlike in Ajaccio – the emphasis in Bastia is on commerce rather than tourism. But despite – or perhaps because of – that, it's got a pleasantly buzzy feel, with around 40,000 permanent residents, and is a very attractive town. It's also got one of the busiest fishing ports in the French Mediterranean, and is a good base for launching into Cap Corse.

The town itself is structured around two main centres – the northern Terra Vecchia (the Old Quarter), with its bustling Old Port, and to the south, the raised Terra Nova (New Quarter) around the Citadel. If you're unlucky, there can be lots of rain and even some pretty violent storms in Bastia, but the locals keep the rare bad weather at bay with a steady stream of music and food festivals, invariably celebrating the traditions of the island. And who can really complain: they get 340 days of sunshine a year on average.

Bastia was the capital of Corsica when the island was under Genoese rule, and it was the Genoese in the 16th century who built the fortified Citadel (or *bastiglia*) from which the city takes its name. The city breeds many supporters for Corsican independence – the main shopping road, Boulevard Paoli, is named after the man who drove the independence movement in the 1700s (like Bonaparte, you can pretty much lay money on finding one of these in every town).

If you're looking for somewhere to park along Rue Napoléon or Boulevard Pasquale Paoli, be prepared for a wait, as there are often traffic jams along these two busy roads. Better to park up in (paying) Place Saint Nicolas – which is one of Europe's biggest squares, by the way – and walk for a few minutes into Terra Vecchia.

BEACHES

Probably the closest beach is just south of town, **Plage de l'Arinella**, which has plenty of watersports, and not far away to the north are **Toga** and **Pietranera**. Basically, if you just head along the corniche road of

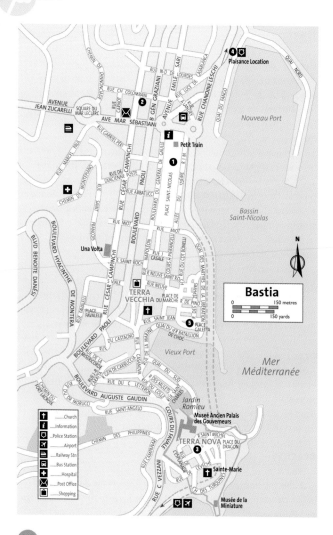

Bastia

Legend:
- Church
- Information
- Police Station
- Airport
- Railway Stn
- Bus Station
- Hospital
- Post Office
- Shopping

Mioma to the north of Bastia, you'll be inundated with sand. The Nature Reserve of Biguglia isn't far away either.

Biguglia Nature Reserve
Just past Marana Beach, this nature reserve centres around the Biguglia Lake. It might not be so good for sunbathing, but is great for fishing!

Corniche of Miomo
A 24-km (15-mile) stretch of road (D31), the corniche starts at Toga Beach and Pietranera, and then snakes upwards, clinging to the coast. You'll pass through the village of Miomo, where a small stony beach with rock pools is fun for children to poke around in, then on to San-Martino-di-Lota, from where there is an amazing view over the valley.

Plage de la Marana
Six miles (10 km) south of town, Marana Beach is lined with trees and cafés, and is a good place for boating, windsurfing and body-boarding – or stay on land and try mini-golf or tennis.

THINGS TO SEE & DO

A gaggle of café owners, fishermen, hawkers and tourists make the port a lively place day and night. The port itself is surrounded by old buildings with a rundown charm (unemployment in Bastia runs at 20 per cent, although you wouldn't know it). There's a 15th-century Citadel that is almost entirely intact, and at night the whole city is lit up. Every October, Bastia holds a festival of jazz, blues and world music called Les Musicales de Bastia.

Église Ste-Marie
This is a large 15th-century church with a Virgin made of solid silver.
ⓐ Terra Nova 🕐 08.00–12.00 & 14.00–18.30 daily, summer; 08.00–12.00 & 14.00–17.30 daily, winter

Musée de la Miniature

This is a miniature recreation of a traditional Corsican village.
ⓐ Near La Citadelle ⓣ 06 10 26 82 08/04 95 38 27 99 ⓦ www.eco-musee.com ⓛ 09.00–12.00 & 14.00–18.00 daily, Mar–Oct ⓝ For information call Bastia Buses (ⓣ 04 95 31 06 65 ⓦ www.bastiabus.com) ⓘ Admission charge

Le Petit Train

This tourist train ride around the town lasts 45 minutes and goes along rue Napoléon, the Citadel and right through the Old Town.
ⓐ Place St Nicolas ⓣ 04 95 35 40 20

Terra Vecchia (Old Town)

The Old Town is full of tightly spiralling streets centred around the Hôtel de Ville (where a market is held daily except Monday). At weekends, markets keep going but just change location – the Place du Marché holds a flower and clothing market on Saturday and Sunday mornings, and you can find Corsican goats' cheeses and *brébis* (cheese made from raw sheep's milk) as well as local charcuterie in the open market in Cours Pierangeli.

For traditional Coriscan goods, from cheeses and wines to dried meats and olive oil, try **U Muntagnolu** ⓐ 15 rue César Campinchi ⓣ 04 95 32 78 04 ⓛ 09.00–12.30 & 14.00–08.00 Mon–Sat

Una Volta

This is Bastia's cultural centre, which runs music and drama workshops for children and grown-ups, holds numerous exhibitions, and hosts an annual Comic Strip Festival in April.
ⓐ Arcades du Théâtre, rue César Campinchi ⓣ 04 95 32 12 81 ⓔ centreculturel@una-volta.org ⓦ www.una-volta.org ⓝ Line 2 goes down Boulevard Paoli, from where you can walk

◆ *Bastia's Old Port by the Terra Vecchia*

TAKE A BREAK

Bars & cafés
Head for Place Saint Nicolas at night, where things start getting lively around 20.00 or 21.00.

Boulangerie du Marché £ ❶ Mainly a drop-in boulangerie, but with a few tables. Try their pizzas made with local cheeses. ⓐ Place St Nicolas ❶ 04 95 31 61 19 ⓛ 06.00–21.00 daily

Raugi Serge £ ❷ An ice-cream parlour with a great range of flavours, in the best Italian tradition. In winter, you get pizza instead of ice cream. ⓐ 2 bis rue Chanoine-Colombani ❶ 04 95 31 22 31 ⓛ 09.00–02.00 Tues–Sun, May–Sept; 09.00–22.00, Oct–Apr

AFTER DARK

Restaurants
A Casarella ££ ❸ A small and simple restaurant with a lovely terrace serving traditional Corsican food, including a lethal *brocciu* (local cheese) and eau-de-vie dessert. Plenty of loyal customers, so you need to book ahead. ⓐ Rue de Ste-Croix ❶ 04 95 32 02 32 ⓛ 12.00–14.00 & 19.00–22.30 Mon–Fri; 19.00–22.30 Sat & Sun

La Corniche ££ ❹ This is a hotel with a great restaurant, open to non-guests, and really well worth making the drive to visit: it sits high above the sea and has huge windows overlooking the waves. ⓐ San Martino di Lota ❶ 04 95 31 40 98 ❶ 04 95 32 37 69 ⓦ www.hotel-lacorniche.com ⓛ 12.00–14.00 & 19.00–22.00 Tue eve–Sun

Clubs
U Fanale ££ ❺ Fantastic musical evenings, everything from Cuban swing to traditional Corsican singers. This is a really great fun venue. ⓐ Place Galetta ❶ 04 95 32 68 38 ⓛ 22.00–05.00, closed Christmas

Corte

For a break from beaches, pack some hiking boots along with your swimsuit and head for the hills. The Parc Naturel Régional runs down the centre of Corsica, almost for its entire length, and Corte is the perfect base for exploring it. It stands about 64 km (40 miles) from Ajaccio at the outlet of several rivers, including the Restonica, meaning it is good for kayaking. A well-surfaced but very narrow road, the D623, winds through the Gorge de la Restonica to the town.

This independent town lies right at the heart of Corsican nationalism. For a short time in the 18th century it was the capital of Pascal Paoli's Corsican state (so yes, the main street here is Cours Paoli). It now has a good university, a large Citadel, some narrow cobbled streets and the Musée de la Corse. Shopping and eating are mainly concentrated around Cours Paoli, and the food here is unsurprisingly dominated by meat rather than fish – and the ever-present Corsican cheese, because we are deep in shepherd country here. Oh, and there are chestnuts. Lots of them.

A few miles to the southwest, walkers will find a number of glacial lakes and natural gorges (head down to Vallée de la Restonica for this). There's no need to stop swimming just because you don't have the sea – there are plenty of bitingly cold mountain lakes to jump into!

Buses and trains connect Corte with Ajaccio, Bastia and other towns on the island.

THINGS TO SEE & DO

Most of the craft industries are centred around Castagniccia (to the northeast of Corte, with lots of wooden objects from the many chestnut trees). In Corte itself, Cours Paoli has a market and an animated atmosphere, with its cafés, restaurants and shops selling local produce.

It's also worth knowing that at Bocognano, another inland town, there is the biggest regional fair in Corsica. It is held every December: a chestnut fair that attracts over 20,000 visitors trying everything from chestnut liqueurs to chestnut jams. It has been designated a 'Site remarquable du Goût' (a place where tastes of special interest can be enjoyed). While driving around, look out for tiny drystone houses known as 'pagliaghju'.

Musée de la Corse

This museum hosts three permanent exhibitions: on the history of Corsica, on its traditions and economy, and on the well-preserved battlements in Corte. It also has very interesting visiting exhibits, for example on the history of tourism on the island.

ⓐ La Citadelle ① 04 95 45 25 45 ① 04 95 45 25 36
ⓔ info@musee-corse.com ⓦ www.musee-corse.com ① 10.00–17.45 daily, June–Sept; closed Mon, Oct; closed Sun & Mon, Nov–Mar
① Admission charge

Musée Pasquale Paoli

This may not be so popular with tourists, perhaps, but it is a place of pilgrimage for Corsicans and is set to be enlarged. The bicentenary of Paoli's death is being commemorated in 2007.

ⓐ Hameau Stretta, Morosaglia ① 04 95 61 04 97 ① 09.00–18.00 daily, May–Sept; 9.00–15.00 daily, Oct–Apr

---

STRAW HOUSES

The *pagliaghju* dwellings that can be found in this area were built by shepherds in the late 19th and early 20th centuries. Their name derives from the Corsican for straw, because they were originally used to store and dry out grass and grain for the animals. Sometimes they were used as a place where the farmers could pound corn into flour and dry out cheeses when they had been made. They also served as protection for the shepherd – and his flocks too – when the weather was bad. There are thousands of these small dwellings dotted around the agricultural areas of the island.

TAKING A BREAK

Bars & cafés

This is the Castagniccia (chestnut) region, so expect to be sampling plenty of them. Two of the island's signature dishes come from here: chestnut polenta and five-meat lasagne.

Pâtisserie Casanova Prestige £ Don't go to Corte without stocking up on Corsican pastries, made with chestnut flour, from this delicious bakery. ⓘ 6 cours Paoli ⓣ 04 95 46 00 79 ⓛ 07.30–19.30 Mon–Sat; 07.30–12.30 Sun

AFTER DARK

Restaurants

A Scudella ££ Right in the heart of Corte, Corsican specialities, so lots of charcuterie, ravioli *brocciu* (the local cheese), wild boar and roast duck. ⓐ 2 place Paoli ⓣ 04 95 46 25 31 ⓛ 12.00–14.30 & 19.00–22.00 daily

⬤ Corte lies in the Parc Naturel Régional de Corse

Bars

Bar L'Oriente £ Popular local bar with all-day service and a friendly owner. ⓐ 5 avenue Jean Nicoli ① 04 95 61 11 77 ⓛ 06.30–21.00 daily (but it depends on the crowd: on Saturday nights has been known to stay open until 02.00)

🔺 *Vivario lies high in the hills near Corte*

Porto-Vecchio

The third biggest town on Corsica, and one of the biggest tourist draws, Porto-Vecchio is easily reached by air and sea, and is on the coastal road between Bastia and Bonifacio, overlooking the Gulf of Porto-Vecchio. An old Genoese walled town, Porto-Vecchio is also a popular Italian tourist resort, which means you start eating and partying late here, far more so than in the 'French-style' resorts on the island. There are plenty of upscale boutiques, art galleries and cheerful restaurants lining the winding narrow streets that lead down to the harbour, and there is a generally chic but lively atmosphere. Porto-Vecchio also has one of the latest and most varied nightlife scenes on the island. As with many fortified Corsican towns, you're best to leave your car at the marina and take the little tourist train up to the higher part of town.

There are a number of buses linking Porto-Vecchio with the other big towns on the island, and to the local beaches. Les Rapides Bleu ⓐ Rue Jean Jaurès, 20137 Porto-Vecchio ⓘ 04 95 70 96 52 ⓕ 04 95 70 96 55 Ⓝ Lines 1 and 2 do the local routes

BEACHES

The Gulf of Porto-Vecchio has an excellent range of beaches, from **Cala Rossa** to **Palombaggia**, **Saint Cyprien** and **Santa Giulia** – all within 15 km (less than 10 miles) of Porto-Vecchio.

For information on a bus that takes you to Santa Giulia beach ⓘ 04 95 70 10 36

Plage de Palombaggia
One of the best on the island, the water is shallow and safe for little ones, and there are pine trees along the back of the beach for a fragrant backdrop. It might get a bit overcrowded in the high summer, but if you're lucky enough to be there off season, this is pure beach dynamite.

Plage de Rondinara
This is the one regularly featured on postcards – it's picture-perfect pretty, and usually quieter than the other beaches around Porto-Vecchio.

Plage de Santa Giulia
More fine white sand and clear blue waters, you could almost be in the Caribbean here. This beach also has plenty of cafés and snack bars, and a busy watersports centre.

THINGS TO SEE & DO

Get up late, siesta in the afternoon, and dance until the early hours. But if you do want to squeeze in a bit of sightseeing as well...

Citadelle
The Old Town here is cut through by Cours Napoléon, and the liveliest part is around Place de la République, with its shaded cafés. There are also some ancient fortifications – wander up Rue Borgo for a good look from the battlements down to the port.

TAKING A BREAK

Cafés line the Place de la République.

AFTER DARK

Restaurants
Le Bistrot £–££ Chef Sylvain Piguet cooks up fish, fish and more fish (they even have their own full-time fisherman). Centrally located with a good terrace, and often live saxophone or piano at night. This is probably the best place in the port. ⓐ Quai Pascal Paoli, Port de Plaisance
ⓣ 04 95 70 22 96 ⓕ 04 95 72 20 54 ⓛ Daily, June–Sept; Mon–Sat, Oct–Jan & Mar–June; closed Feb

Le Donjon ££ Just by Cours Napoléon, this lovely restaurant has a limited but well-chosen menu, with inventive takes on local food, and a few more international dishes as well. ⓐ 5 rue Paul Ciabrini ⓣ 06 30 72 72 60 ⓛ Year round, but closed lunchtime Thur–Sun in winter

Clubs
Via Notte ££ Nightclub with restaurant attached. ⓐ Zone industrielle Mortone ⓣ 04 95 72 02 12 ⓕ 04 95 72 02 13 ⓛ 21.00 (dinner); 23.00–04.00 (club), May–Sept

🔺 *Porto-Vecchio's tranquil harbour*

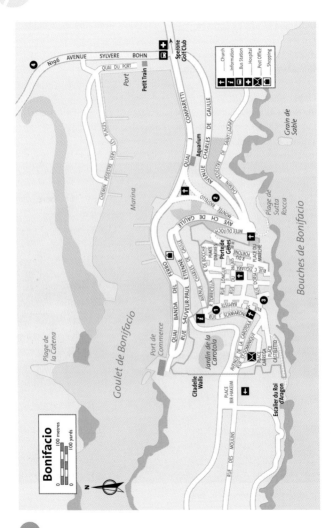

Bonifacio

Bonifacio

If you had only one day, and one choice, you should make a trip to this town. Bonifacio is not only completely gorgeous – perched on a cliff, enclosed by fortified walls, impossibly picturesque – it is also a great starting point for some excellent trips. It sits right up on top of a limestone peninsula at Corsica's southernmost tip, nose to nose with the Italian island of Sardinia, which lies less then 16 km (10 miles) away.

The very best thing about Bonifacio is the way you get into the (carefully restored) walled part of the city. You have to clamber through a centuries-old entrance, stepping through walls and an arched door that are about 1.25 m (4 ft) thick. Inside the walls, it's an endless maze of narrow lanes twisting up to the Citadel. There's good shopping here, with local crafts and silver jewellery on offer (coral jewellery as well, although you won't be allowed to bring it back to the UK). There's also a maritime cemetery, at the edge of town overlooking the sea.

There are two distinct parts to Bonifacio – down on the lower level around the port, and the top section, up on the cliff, where the Citadel stands. There's a tourist train that runs between the two. Or, if you're feeling up to it, you can take the stairs – the Rastello and St Roch steps (the original ones are still visible in the cliffs, but not advised on account of their being death-defyingly steep and without a handrail). If you're driving, there's a car park down by the port, and another up in the Old Town. ⚠ There's a bus that runs between Porto-Vecchio and Bonifacio ☎ 04 95 70 13 83, but no local buses once you're there

BEACHES

The actual coastline directly below the town is dramatically craggy, and exploring it makes for a great way of spending the day, either picking your way along the shoreline, or going by boat. Children are going to love exploring the grottoes and secret coves. And of course there are plenty of boat trips to nearby beaches, the **Plages de Bonifacio**, especially Cala di Paragnano and Plage de la Tonnara.

Cala di Paragnano

Take the N196 just a few miles from Bonifacio and you'll find a beach that could have been whisked straight from Thailand, with white sand, red rocks and crystal-clear water.

Plage de Santa Manza

This is a great sandy beach in the Gulf of Santa Manza, which has some of the best windsurfing on the island. Take the D58 to the east of Bonifacio.

THINGS TO SEE & DO

Aquarium de Bonifacio

There are some natural caves in this aquarium that make it especially interesting, and plenty of local fish. ⓐ 71 quai Comparetti
ⓣ and ⓕ 04 95 73 03 69

Citadelle

You don't just visit a Citadel during your stay in Bonifacio – the whole place is basically one big Citadel, so you get the full-on immersion experience. The 'high town' has an interesting monument to the Foreign Legion, the Church of St Dominique, and there are some great shops selling traditional Corsican products – both food and crafts.

To stock up on charcuterie, honeys and wines, try **Roba Nosta**
ⓐ 15 rue Doria ⓣ 04 95 73 12 56 ⓦ www.bonifacio.com/roba
ⓛ 09.00–19.00 daily, July & Aug, 09.00–12.00 & 15.00–18.30 daily, Sept–June; closed Jan–Feb

Petit Train Touristique

The ride takes 35 minutes from top to bottom.
ⓐ Parking down by the port ⓣ 04 95 73 15 07 ⓛ 09.00–24.00 July–Aug, 09.00–18.00 Apr–June, Sept & Oct ⓘ Admission charge

Sperone Golf Club
The only 18-hole course on the island, recently voted one of the best in
Europe, with impressive views. Good restaurant also for non-golf-playing
friends and family. ⓐ Domaine de Sperone ⓣ 04 95 73 17 13
ⓦ www.sperone.com

🔺 *Bonifacio's Citadelle towers over the port*

◯ *One of the ancient narrow streets near the Citadelle*

TAKING A BREAK

Cafés
Boulangerie Faby £ ❶ Lots of local specialities, from an orange-infused galette to a walnut and raisin brioche. ⓐ 4 rue St Jean Baptiste
ⓣ 04 95 73 14 73 ⓛ 06.30–19.00

AFTER DARK

Restaurants
U Campanile £ ❷ On the way to the Citadel, opposite the church of Saint-Erasme, this has good simple pizzas and salads. ⓐ 7 montée Rastello ⓣ 04 95 73 09 10 ⓛ 12.00–15.00 & 19.00–22.00, closed Dec–Feb.

Stella D'Oro ££ ❸ Good local specialities, which basically means plenty of grilled fish. ⓐ 7 rue Doria ⓣ 04 95 73 93 63 ⓔ stella.ora@bonifacio.com
ⓛ 12.00–14.00 & 19.00–22.00 daily, but closed Oct–Apr

Au Jardin D'Acheda £££ ❹ Gastronomic restaurant that is not just for hotel guests. The chef Sebastien Mortet is from Dijon and, although this is expensive food, it is memorable. Save room for the desserts.
ⓐ Cavallo Morto ⓣ 04 95 73 03 02 ⓦ www.acheda-hotel.com

Clubs
There are lots of nightclubs and late-night bars all the way from Bonifacio to Porto-Vecchio, but you'll be pretty well entertained just down by the harbour in Bonifacio itself.

Propriano

Almost exactly halfway between Ajaccio and Bonifacio, this is possibly the town on the island most changed by the influx of tourists. It really wasn't that long ago that Propriano was a tiny, unfinished fishing port, and it still has a natural harbour with a slightly rustic feel. But its setting in the Valinco Gulf, its numerous wide sandy beaches and its gently shelving coastline meant that it would never stay undiscovered for long – even if sometimes, early in the morning, you can still believe that you can keep this all to yourself.

The modern-day resort town of Propriano is busy, but not overwhelming, and is appropriated more by families than the international designer sunglasses set. The many restaurants and bars are child-friendly, and within just the one stretch of beach in the town, you can organise anything from sailing to paragliding.

There are not too many local buses here – but there are links with Porto-Vecchio and Bonifacio. Information from Ecocorse Voyages, ⓐ Gare Routière, 20000 Ajaccio ⓣ 04 95 21 06 30

BEACHES

There are a number that are within easy walking distance of the town centre, and plenty more within a short drive.

Olmeto Plage
Big tourist beach with good white sands, lots of camping, restaurants and watersports. It lies 10 km (6$\frac{1}{4}$ miles) to the west of Propriano and there are three buses a day (see page 69).

Plage du Corsaire
Really an extension of Lido Beach, the sand becomes deeper and more attractive here, and there are lifeguards stationed here in July and August, which makes this a better bet for families.

Plage du Lido

This is behind the busy commercial port, marked out by the Scoglio Longo lighthouse.

THINGS TO SEE & DO

Scuba diving, snorkelling, boat rides: a lot of the fun here is centred round water. Le Port de Plaisance is the centre of much of it. In town, there's a fruit and vegetable market held daily.

Aztech Marine

On the pretty Santa Giulia beach – everything from scuba diving to jet skiing. ⓐ Baie de Santa Giulia, route du Moby Dick. ❶ 04 95 70 22 67
ⓦ www.divecorsica.com ❷ 09.00–19.00, Apr–Oct

Valinco Plongée

One of the many diving centres along the beach front and port.
ⓐ Port de Plaisance ❶ 04 95 76 31 01 ⓦ www.valinco-plongee.com
❷ Daily by appointment, Apr–Oct

🔺 *Idyllic Olmeto Plage*

TAKING A BREAK

Bars & restaurants

There is a wide choice of eating and drinking places; they are mainly centred around Quai Saint Erasme and the Porte de Plaisance.

Au Péché Mignon £ Start your day at this *salon de thé* nestling among the other bars along the port. Their chestnut gâteaux are not to be missed! ⓐ 5 avenue Napoléon ⓣ 04 95 76 01 71 ⓛ 08.30–19.00

AFTER DARK

Restaurants

Auberge San Ghjuvani ££ If you have had enough of fish, and want a night back on traditional Corsican cuisine, this is the place to come – about 10 minutes inland from Propriano, towards Vetaro. Veal, snails and cannelloni stuffed with *brocciu* cheese are often on the menu, and every Friday in summer they run 'Corsican Nights' when there is traditional singing and dancing. Good fun. ⓐ Plaine Barracci Monaca, Viggianello ⓣ 04 95 76 03 31 ⓕ 04 95 76 21 55 ⓛ 12.00–14.00 & 19.30–21.30 (later in summer)

La Tout Va Bien (Chez Parenti) ££ The name means everything is going well – and indeed it has here for over 80 years! Located right opposite the port. ⓐ 13 avenue de Napoléon ⓣ 04 95 76 12 14 ⓛ 12.00–14.00 & 19.00–23.00; closed Jan to Mar

Le Lido ££ This serves mainly seafood – and the location, perched on top of a cliff, means that you can watch the fish being caught. ⓐ Avenue de Napoléon ⓣ 04 95 76 06 37 ⓛ 12.00–14.00 & 19.00–22.00 Mon–Sat

● *Cliff formations near Bonifacio*

EXCURSIONS
Out & about

Excursions
in the south

0	10 km
0	8 miles

Excursions in the south

Les Îles Sanguinaires

Four small islands in the Gulf of Ajaccio, and a good destination for boat trips. The reason they are so dramatically known as the 'blood-red islands' is because of the gorgeous red colour they take on at sunset, rather than for any blood-curdling past – although there have been plenty of pirates around here during the island's history, so feel free to make up your own more romantic alternative. The islands lie just off Pointe de la Parata (the other direction out of Ajaccio from Porticcio), where there are more walks and beautiful coastal scenery.

🅝 Of course, getting to these islands by boat is ideal – you can organise this from Ajaccio. There are a number of boats for hire all along the quays, but try: **Nave Va** (ⓐ Quai Napoléon ❶ 04 95 21 83 97 🅦 www.naveva.com). The D111 takes you to Tour de la Parata, from where the boats go to the islands

THINGS TO SEE & DO

Your day starts as you're leaving Ajaccio along the Routes des Sanguinaires. This coastal route on the way to the La Parata Point was built in the 19th century when tourism was just beginning to develop, and the best stop is at the Chapelle des Grecs, a church built in the 17th century and dedicated to Santa Maria del Carmine.

The islands are a sanctuary for birds, rare fauna and flora, and offer some private swimming spots and good walking. The biggest island, Grande Sanguinaire, is also the furthest away. Look out for its lighthouse.

TAKING A BREAK

Restaurants
There are no eating and drinking places on the islands themselves; these are strictly scenic spots to take photos and gasp in delight at the sunsets,

not for landing on and grabbing a pint. But there are a few decent restaurants on the drive up towards them, where you get the view.

L'Ariadne Plage £ In summer, you sometimes get impromptu concerts and musical evenings on the beach in front of the restaurant. But whenever you go, you'll get good music, a mix of Asian-influenced food, pizzas and huge fish barbecues. ⓐ Route Îles des Sanguinaires ⓘ 04 95 52 09 63 ⓛ 12.00–15.00, 19.00–23.00; closed Nov–Jan ⓝ Nos 1 and 2 buses go from Ajaccio to Îles Sanguinaires (ⓣ 04 95 23 29 41)

I Sanguinari £ This used to be a fish restaurant, but has recently converted to a brasserie, *salon de thé*, and souvenir shop. The food is cheerful if not exactly mind-blowing, but it does come complete with *that* view – you'd better book ahead if you want a table to coincide with sunset. La Parata, route Îles des Sanguinaires ⓣ 04 95 52 01 70 ⓘ 04 95 52 07 42 ⓛ 09.00–21.00 July & Aug; 09.00–18.30 Sept–June ⓝ Nos 1 and 2 buses go from Ajaccio to Îles Sanguinaires (ⓣ 04 95 23 29 41)

Filitosa

The best of the many prehistoric sites scattered across Corsica, about 18 km (11 miles) north of Propriano, and about 40 km (25 miles) south of Ajaccio. This one has clear remains from Neolithic times (when basically everyone on the island was a shepherd or farmer), Megalithic (still shepherds and farmers, but burying their dead and doing more sophisticated hunting), Torean (from 1600–800 BC, which is when many of the fortresses were first built) and Roman (who left their imprint on Corsica every bit as much as they did elsewhere in Europe). The site was first discovered in 1946.

ⓝ You will need your own transport to get here; there is no public transport. There is a little car park in the village of Filitosa where you can leave your vehicle. The archaeological site is about a 15-minute walk from there

THINGS TO SEE & DO

Frankly, you really only come to Filitosa for one thing, and that's the archaeological tour. If you have children, look out for the caves to keep them occupied.

🔺 *Filitosa is famous for its prehistoric statue-menhirs*

Archaeological site

There's a one-hour guided visit and some very interesting walks to do. The site boasts many structures that are still a bit of a mystery to archaeologists, including Megalithic menhir statues, basically carved-out human faces in full battle cry, as well as circular stone *torri*, which might have been for worship, and hut platforms. Oh, and some good caves that date back to 3300 BC, and even a 1,200-year-old olive tree. A small museum offers further menhirs, as well as some ancient tools and pottery found in the caves.

(t) 04 95 74 00 91 **(L)** 08.00–sundown daily, Apr–Oct **(N)** No direct transport: the closest is to Propriano with Alta Rocca Voyages from the SNCF station (**(t)** 04 95 51 08 19) **(i)** Admission charge

Tip: There are lots of olive groves in this area, so look out for roadside stalls selling bottles of olive oil.

Auberge du Domaine Comte Abbatucci

A friendly *ferme auberge* (farm with restaurant and rooms), plenty of local produce and home-made olive oil. They also produce and sell a good local wine.

(a) Pont de Calzola, Casalabriva **(t)** 04 95 24 36 30 **(L)** 12.00–14.00 & 18.00–20.00, closed Oct–Mar **(N)** No buses, but by car it's 7 km (4¹/₂ miles) north of Filitosa, on the D457

Gulf of Valinco

The Gulf of Valinco has the oldest history on the island. To the north of the bay is Cappiciolo, full of picturesque coves and dusky red rocks. The main stopping place here is Porto-Pollo, at the northern end of the gulf. Heading the other way, travellers cross the Rizzanese river (where it is delightful to stop and swim), to go down to Belvédère and Campomoro. **(N)** Porto-Pollo is about three hours' journey north from Propriano, on the D757. Belvédère and Campomoro are south of Propriano on the D121, a shorter distance from Propriano, taking about one and a half hours

THINGS TO SEE & DO

On offer are waterskiing and windsurfing, sailing and scuba diving. And heading inland there is even more: horse-riding, hiking, walking and also climbing are all possible. There are even some microlight flights on offer!

Asinudi Figuccia

Donkey rides! Well, in fact this really involves walking, with a mule carrying your baggage and/or children. It lasts either one hour, half a day, or a whole day. It's a great way to see the country, though, and may be enough to persuade younger family members that walking can be fun.
ⓐ Route de Maggiese, Olmeto Plage ① 06 03 28 92 00/06 03 28 81 85
🕒 09.00–13.00 & 17.00–20.0, Mar–Sept

Baracci Hot Springs

The Rizzanese river has rock pools and river swimming – and at Baracci there are hot springs, which have been used since Roman times. The source was capped in the late 19th century and the waters are supposed to cure a range of ailments.

Établissements des Sources de Baracci (Bains de Baracci)

These were ancient Roman baths, known for their healing properties. Today visitors can wallow in a hot water pool, spa, Jacuzzi – all sheer heaven.
ⓐ Olmeto Plage ① 04 95 76 30 40 🕒 09.00–12.00 & 15.00–20.00, June–Sept; 09.00–12.00 & 15.00–19.00, Oct–May

Parcours d'arbre en arbre de Baracci (Baracci Tree Adventure)

The Tree Adventure is another enormously child-friendly activity. The kids get to swing up in the trees, walking across tightropes strung 10 m (33 ft) up in the air. Adults might pretend they want to join them, but are probably happy to leave this one to the braver members of the family.
ⓐ Monaca, Viggianello ① 06 20 95 45 34 ⓔ skaladkamel@hotmail.fr
🕒 09.00–19.00, mid-June–mid-Sept

Tip: The southernmost point of this gulf is at Campomoro. It's a bit of a hike, but you see some amazing rock formations, white and round, with sections missing, like a line of Polo mints. And if you've made it this far, there's also a deserted white-sand beach to reward your efforts.

TAKING A BREAK

Restaurants

It depends which way you head out of Propriano – there are more restaurants on the D157 road to Porto-Pollo, but you'll still find a few great spots the other way, heading off to Campomoro.

U Farniente ££ If you were considering whether to bother making the trip to Olmeto Plage, this restaurant alone makes it worthwhile, not just for the food (fish, and lots of it), but for the views back over Propriano. ⓐ Arcobiato, Olmeto Plage ⓣ 04 95 74 07 48 ⓛ 12.00–14.00 & 19.00–22.00

Alta Rocca

Alta Rocca, which means 'high rocks' in Corsican, is breathtaking.

THINGS TO SEE & DO

Horse-riding

This is wonderful country to see from the back of a horse. Rides depart from Ste Lucie de Porto-Vecchio.
Country Horse ⓐ Lieu dit Bacca ⓣ 06 11 99 45 93

La Musée de l'Alta Rocca, Levie

This museum houses collections sourced mainly from archaeological excavations conducted at Alta Rocca since 1963. From May 2007 the museum will be enlarged and have longer opening hours.

ⓐ Musée Levie, Avenue Lieutenant Aviateur De Peretti, Levie
ⓣ 04 95 78 46 34 ⓕ 04 95 78 41 60 ⓔ musee.levie@cg-corsedusud.fr
ⓦ www.cg-corsedusud.fr ⓛ 13.00–17.00 Mon; 09.00–12.00 &
13.30–17.00 Tues–Sat (longer hours from May 2007)

Bavella

This is a world-renowned walking spot and forest. The Col de Bavella lies
at 1,218 m (3,996 ft). The views from here are spectacular: best in
springtime, when the heather is purple and the whole place smells of
thyme. There's also an auberge up on the mountain, and a recently
opened Maison d'Acceuil, which has a large car park.
ⓝ Take the N196 from Propriano but turn off at Sartène on the D69,
then take the D420 to Bavella. It takes about 90 minutes from
Propriano. Alternatively, start from Porto-Vecchio, from where you can
take the N198, then almost immediately pick up the D368 to Bavella.
Both routes involve small, windy roads

TAKING A BREAK

Restaurants
La Pergola ££ Right in the centre of Levie, they can hardly squeeze more
than ten people in this restaurant – but if you are one of the 10, count
yourself lucky, because it's great food and very well priced. ⓣ 04 95 78
41 62 ⓛ 12.00–14.00 & 19.00–23.00, closed Nov–Apr

Sartène and the Vallée de l'Ortolo

This is the spot to come for truly deserted roads and secret walking trails.
There's also a horse-riding centre for discovering them all if you don't
want to walk. This was once a major wine-growing area (there are still a
few vineyards), until Phylloxera struck; nowadays the valley feels wild and

abandoned. The town of Sartène itself, built like an amphitheatre into the hills, fervently keeps alive some of Corsica's oldest traditions, such as the *Catenacciu*, a Good Friday procession re-enacting the crucifixion. The narrow streets are lined with tall, fortress-like houses that could be barricaded to protect against vendetta. This is particularly evident in the Santa Anna quarter, which still has many bricked-up windows.

🚍 Take the N196 from Propriano direct to Sartène (it only takes around 10 minutes). The valley is further in, eastward, via minor roads, or you can stick to the N196 to get to the Roccapina and the lion rock.

BEACHES

Midway between Bonifacio and Sartène, Roccapina is the most famous beach in the area, mainly for the rocks that are shaped like a lion. But up in Sartène, travellers must get into the spirit of wild Corsica.

🔺 *Vineyards at Sartène*

THINGS TO SEE & DO

Domaine Saparale
Wine maker Philippe Farinelli works here producing very good white wines.
ⓐ 5 cours Bonaparte, Sartène ⓣ 04 95 77 15 13 ⓕ 04 95 73 43 08

Musée Départemental de Préhistoire, Sartène
As you'd expect for a museum located so close to all these Megalithic sites, this traces the daily life of civilisations from the 8th century BC to the beginning of the 1st century AD. Good displays of weapons, costumes, jewellery, vases, tools and menhir statues.
ⓐ Rue Croce, Sartène ⓣ and ⓕ 04 95 77 01 09 ⓔ musee.sartene@cg-corsedusud.fr ⓦ www.cg-corsedusud.fr ⓛ 10.00–17.00

TAKING A BREAK

Restaurants
Chez Antoine ££ Right on the bay at Tizzano, you get good, fresh seafood and plenty of salad to accompany it. Small menu, but you're going to want what they have on offer. ⓐ Port, Tizzano ⓣ 04 95 77 09 06 ⓛ 12.00–14.00 & 18.00–21.00; closed Oct–May

Gulf of Porto-Vecchio

Evidence of people living here dates back to the Bronze Age, and who can blame them, as the whole place is full of tiny bays and sheltered coves. Ⓝ Take the N198 north from Porto-Vecchio and the D468 off it. For the Îles Cerbicale, you will need to take a boat from Porto-Vecchio.

THINGS TO SEE & DO

The beaches are amazing (this is where Palombaggia is), and there are lots of prehistoric sites to find. And don't forget birdwatching.

Les Îles Cerbicale

The Îles Cerbicale comprise 60 hectares (148 acres) of sea, coast and islands; a rare bird sanctuary and one of the best places for spotting cormorants on Corsica.

TAKING A BREAK

Restaurants

La Costa Rica ££ Large windows and a terrace give wonderful views over the bay. The menu changes daily at this restaurant based in the Hôtel Castell'Verde. ⓐ Golfe de Santa Giulia, Porto-Vecchio ❶ 04 95 72 24 51 ❶ 12.00–14.00 & 19.30–22.00 May–Sept

Les Îles Lavezzi

Classified as a nature reserve since 1981, lying in between Corsica and Sardinia, these islands just sneak into French soil and count as the southernmost tip of France. The nature reserve is actually made up of over 100 tiny islands and outcrops, only one of which, Lavezzi, is accessible by the public.

Ⓝ From Bonifacio, there are numerous small boat operators and tour companies that run boats to the Lavezzi islands. A good one is: Rocca Croisières (ⓐ 6 rue Fred Scamaroni, Bonifacio ❶ 04 95 73 13 96 ❶ 04 95 73 15 39 ❷ info@croisieres-bonifacio.com Ⓦ www.rocca-croisieres.com)

THINGS TO SEE & DO

Well, there are no restaurants, bars, cafés, no hotels, not even a toilet, but there is scenery, and lots of it. The islands have been protected from development by strict planning laws – but not from the wind; this has transformed the islands into a crazy granite moonscape, broken up by tiny sandy beaches. Your boat trip from Bonifacio lasts a minimum of three hours. Three ferry companies make the trip from Bonifacio: Rocca

Croisières (rocca-croisieres.com), Vedettes Thalassa (vedettesthalassa.com) and Vedettes Christina (bonifacio.com.fr/christina). And don't miss the last boats back (around 18.30pm – check when you are there).

Tip: Take your snorkelling gear, as the waters are very clear.

Sardinia

If even Porto-Vecchio isn't Italian enough for you, you can easily reach the real thing. Sardinia is just under 16 km (10 miles) from Corsica, and the part you reach most easily is among its most attractive sections – the Maddalena Archipelago and the Costa Smeralda – apparently a coast with the most marinas in the world, where rich Italians park their yachts at well-heeled resorts such as Porto Cervo. And did you know that, in Sardinia, more people live to be 100 or older than anywhere else in the world? Apparently it's due to the diet, so eat up while you're there!

From Bonifacio, it's 50 minutes away by boat to Santa Teresa on Sardinia (www.mobylines.it)

THINGS TO SEE & DO

Sta Teresa di Gallura is the port of arrival; this is about 32 km (20 miles) away from Porto Cervo along the coast road if you are interested in exploring where the seriously wealthy hang out. Sta Teresa is more modest, but it's a pretty harbour town, and for a day trip there's little need to go any further; although there are good buses if you're feeling adventurous and, if you are, the main sightseeing spot is Capo Testa. If you want to take the bus, tickets are on sale at the bus station.

Capo Testa
Just under 7 km (4 miles) from Sta Teresa, this is little more than a rocky outcrop, but its shape is so peculiar that you're going to be glad you made the effort.

A sheltered cove at Capo Testa

Costa Smeralda

Costa Smeralda is best explored by boat; there'll be plenty of places to anchor up and stop for a drink. If you're a strong swimmer, you can do the James Bond bit of swimming into shore.

Food shopping

Nobody can go to Italy, even if only for one day, and return empty-handed. Local specialities include ricotta ravioli with spinach and mint leaves, and a particularly lethal local grappa, flavoured with local herbs.

Tip: Sardinia is a hot destination for Italian tourists as well, so if you're going during the high season, be prepared for crowds – and book the ferry, and maybe a restaurant, too – before you get to the port.

TAKING A BREAK

Restaurants

Among Sardinia's many outstanding culinary specialities is *sa buttariga*, a smoked-mullet caviar, which can be either served as an appetiser or poured over pasta.

La Terrazza ££ Right opposite the port, this has lots of fresh seafood. Install yourself here for a few hours. ⓐ 6 via Vila Glori, La Maddalena ⓣ (39) 07 89 73 53 05 ⓛ 12.30–15.00 & 20.00–24.00 daily, May–Sept; 12.30–15.00 & 20.00–24.00, Mon–Sat, Oct–Apr

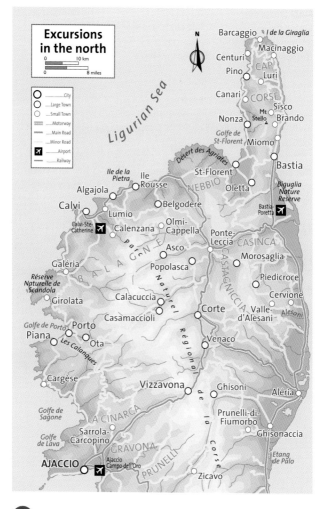

Excursions in the north

| 0 | 10 km |
| 0 | 8 miles |

- ⬭ City
- ⬭ Large Town
- ○ Small Town
- ▭ Motorway
- ▭ Main Road
- ▭ Minor Road
- ✈ Airport
- ▭ Railway

Ligurian Sea

Golfe de St-Florent

Barcaggio · *I de la Giraglia*
Macinaggio
Centuri
Pino · Luri
CAP CORSE
Canari · CORSE
Mt Stello · Sisco
Nonza · Brando
Miomo
Bastia

Désert des Agriates
St-Florent
NEBBIO
Oletta
Biguglia Nature Reserve
Bastia Poretta ✈

Ile de la Pietra · Ile Rousse
Algajola
Calvi
Lumio
Calvi-Ste-Catherine ✈
Calenzana
Belgodere
Olmi-Cappella
Ponte-Leccia
CASINCA
Morosaglia

Galéria
B A L A G N E
Asco
Popolasca
Piedicroce
Cervione
Valle-d'Alesani
Alesani

Réserve Naturelle de Scandola
Girolata
Calacuccia
Casamaccioli
Corte
CASTAGNICCIA

Golfe de Porto
Porto
Piana · Ota
Les Calanques
P a r c
N a t u r e l
R é g i o n a l
Venaco

Cargèse
Vizzavona
Ghisoni
Aléria

Golfe de Sagone
LA CINARCA
Prunelli-di-Fiumorbo
Ghisonaccia

Golfe de Lava
Sarrola-Carcopino
GRAVONA
Etang de Palo

AJACCIO
Ajaccio Campo dell'Oro ✈
PRUNELLI
d e   l a   c o r s e
Zicavo

Excursions in the north

Les Calanques (Les Calanches/The Corniche)

The mass of intriguing red rock formations along the coastal road between Porto and Piana are known as Les Calanques. They are a nerve-racking but memorable highlight of a Corsican holiday.

Les Calanques is situated 2 km (1¹/₄ miles) along the D81 road, south of Porto. Piani village is 348 m (1,142 ft) up, halfway along the Calanche road, and is gorgeous. Ideally you should see the formations from a boat: a good company is **Croisières Grand Bleu** ❸ Route du Puntiglione, Cargèse ❶ 04 95 26 40 24 24 Ⓦ www.croisiere.grandbleu.free.fr

THINGS TO SEE & DO

This is a great area in which to stop the car and do some walking. Best of all is to explore the area by boat, which is easily arranged from Porto.

Le Château Fort

This is a walk of about one hour from the Tête du Chien (where there's a car park), which provides spectacular views out over the sea. It looks out over the whole Gulf of Porto, the tower of Capo Rosso and the Gulf of Girolata. Take your camera, because you're going to want to remember this when you get home.

Tip: Try to do this drive in the late afternoon when the colours of the rocks look their prettiest – and you don't have the overhead sun getting in your eyes during a particularly hair-raising turn. It can get pretty busy in summer.

TAKING A BREAK

There aren't really any stopping-off points here for ready-made food, but take a picnic so that you can linger at one of the many viewpoints.

Girolata

This is a tiny village on the Gulf of Porto, only connected to the rest of the gulf by a mule track. It has a highly intermittent electricity and telephone service but is famous for its langoustines and its seafood restaurants. The vivid red of the rocks that surround it just adds to the dreamlike quality of the whole place. It comprises a short stretch of stony beach, a few houses, a watchtower and not much else.

🄽 Take the D81 north from Porto until just past the Col de la Croix and Osani and you'll see signs for the path where you start walking. Or you can reach it by boat from Porto 🅆 www.croisiere.grandbleu.free.fr

⬥ *The spectacular Calanques road*

THINGS TO SEE & DO

Why not walk up an appetite, then eat it off? The head of the Girolata trail is at **Bocca a Croce** (Col de la Croix), on the Calvi to Porto road, from where a small track heads downhill through forest to a tiny cove known as **Cala di Tuara**. From there it's about a half-hour walk on to Girolata.

TAKING A BREAK

Restaurants
Le Bon Espoir £ More delicious seafood. No credit cards. ☎ 04 95 10 04 55/04 95 22 73 95 🕐 12.00–21.00, May–Oct

La Cabane du Berger £ Offers bed and half board, but also a restaurant. ☎ 04 95 20 16 98 🕐 12.00–22.00, May–Oct

Le Bel Ombra ££ Terrace overlooking the beach. Try their fresh Scandola lobster. ☎ 04 95 22 76 97 🕐 12.00–14.00 & 19.00–22.00, May–Oct ❶ No credit cards.

Tip: In winter, there really is very little open here, so if you want to do the walk, take your own provisions.

Réserve Naturelle de Scandola (Scandola Nature Reserve)

A UNESCO World Heritage Site since 1983, and one to put at the top of your 'must-see' list in Corsica. Scandola stands at 560 m (1,837 ft), between Punta Rossa to the south and Punta Nera to the north, stretching between Porto and Galéria for almost 1,000 hectares (2,471 acres) on the land, and a further 800 hectares (1,977 acres) in the sea. Some of the last ospreys in the Mediterranean have been spotted here, as have peregrine falcons and bearded vultures.

It's only approachable by boat from Calvi, Porto, Propriano or Ajaccio. Visitors can see as they are approaching that most of the coves along the way are partially hidden and that it would be very dangerous to attempt to land

THINGS TO SEE & DO

There is excellent scuba diving off Scandola (you need to organise this back in Calvi) and kayaking in the Gulf of Galéria. This is the clearest water on the island, and you'll see good coral and a mixture of fish.

Tip: Look out for buzzards, cormorants and even puffins.

● *Get away from it all at Cala di Tuara*

TAKING A BREAK

Restaurants
A Mandria, Pont de Solenzara £ This is a comfy little restaurant specialising in mixed grills. ⓐ Scaffa Rossa, Solaro (on the N198) ⓒ 04 95 57 41 95 ⓒ 12.00–14.30 & 19.30–24.00 Mon eve–Sun lunch; closed mid-Jan–mid-Mar ⓝ The bus from Bastia to Porto-Vecchio stops at Solaro

Alesani

This valley lies halfway down the road to Porto-Vecchio from Bastia. It's a stunning corniche road, with hair-raising drops and bends.
ⓝ Take the N198 from Bastia, then the D71 after Santa-Lucia-di-Moriani, and after about 22 km (14 miles) you get to the Alesani Valley

THINGS TO SEE & DO

The village is charming and the lake is a pretty spot for walking and hiking.

Musée Ethnographique de l'Adecéc
This building houses a number of different exhibitions looking at the history and origins of Corsica. There's a recreation of traditional Corsican dwellings on the first floor, and plenty of archaeological treasures.
ⓐ Place Jean Simonetti, Cervione ⓒ 04 95 38 12 83 ⓕ 04 95 38 19 51
ⓦ www.adecec.net ⓒ 10.00–12.00 & 14.30–18.00 Mon–Sat

TAKING A BREAK

Restaurants
L'Auberge du Lac ££ This friendly family-run place is a good reason to go to Alesani. ⓐ Chiatra ⓣ 04 95 38 86 39 ⓒ 12.00–14.00 & 19.00–22.00 daily, May–Oct; the rest of the year by reservation on Fri & Sat only

La Castagniccia

This is chestnut country. They are everywhere: on the trees around and on the plate. And besides chestnuts there is a collection of hills, mountains, steep drops, gorges and tiny villages where a traveller might feel as if they are the first person ever to have wandered into them. The San Petrone mountain is the highest in the region, at 1,767 m (5,797 ft) tall.

It's really not good for public transport around here, so hire a car or a bicycle (take a picnic, too, because there are so many great spots to enjoy). To reach La Castagniccia, take the N193 north from Corte, then follow the road along the Golo river. Minor routes that take you into the heart of the region are the D39, the D71 and the D515

🔺 *Trees cover the hills of La Castagniccia*

THINGS TO SEE & DO

No one can visit this region without coming away feeling just a little bit closer to the humble chestnut. The trees can reach up to 20 m (65 ft) high and are in flower during May and June. And it was those Italians again that marked the area by planting so many chestnut trees in the 15th century.

Away from the trees or, rather, in the middle of them, **Piedicroce** is a fairy-tale village where you have to investigate the gorgeous interior of the **St Pierre et St Paul** church.

The ruins of the 18th-century **Orezza Convent** are worth a look, as are the frescoes of **Chapel San Quilico de Cambia**.

Ponte-Leccia

About 15 minutes from Corte, Ponte-Leccia is the centre of the wool making that still goes on inland. **Lana Corse** makes an excellent visit. There's a small exhibition about the history of textiles in the region and the *brebis* sheep that are native to the island – and plenty of gorgeous wool jumpers, hats and toys to be bought.

ⓐ Route de Saliceto ⓣ 04 95 48 43 79 ⓛ 09.00–19.00 daily, July–Aug; 09.00–18.00 Mon–Fri, Mar–June, Sept–Jan; closed Feb

TAKING A BREAK

Restaurants

Osteria di U Cunventu £ Pascal Paoli was born in this village. Ruminate on his childhood while troughing chestnut dishes at this laid-back restaurant with great views. ⓐ Penteto, Morosaglia ⓣ 04 95 47 11 79 ⓔ cunventu@wanadoo.fr ⓛ 12.00–14.00 Tues–Fri; closed Feb–mid-Mar

La Balagne

Inland from Calvi, this green and hilly region makes fun exploring country. It's getting increasingly popular though – a rash of second-home-owners, tourists and weekending Ajaccians can make it pretty busy in summer. The area sits between the sea and the desert of Agriates, inland from the Gulf of Calvi.

Ⓝ The area is reachable via the D671 (take the N197 north from Calvi or south from l'Île Rousse and then turn off at Algajola). The D151 is a little road that also runs through the Balagne and is very pretty.

THINGS TO SEE & DO

The villages of Calenzana and the evocatively named Lumio are the best destinations, but others include Zilia (famous for its olive oils), Costa (which has a lovely central square), Mur (for cheese, olives and wines) and Pigna (lots of artisans, and particularly well known for its musical instruments).

Calenzana is a small town about 12$\frac{1}{2}$ km (8 miles) from Calvi, with 1,500 inhabitants and lovely architecture. There's a baroque church, the Église Saint Blaise, and the 16th-century Chapel Santa Restituta. Lumio is right above the gulf, so you get sea views here, and a beach, and another gorgeous baroque church.

There are plenty of good local vineyards. Try **Domaine Orsini**, which has a shop and tasting room and sells wines and liqueurs.

ⓣ 04 95 62 81 01 ⓕ 04 95 62 79 70 ⓔ info@domaine-orsini.com
ⓦ www.domaine-orsini.com ⓛ 09.30–12.30 & 14.00–18.00

This is also a horse-riding centre, so saddle up.

Tip: A tourist train goes along the beaches, which is fun for children: it's called 'Le Tramway de Balagne'. Information at the stations at Calvi or l'Île Rousse ⓣ 04 95 60 00 50 ⓛ Apr–Oct

TAKING A BREAK

Restaurants

Le Mata Hari £ Ice-cream parlour and restaurant with a good atmosphere, right on the beach. There's a bar in the evening even when they're not serving food. ❸ Plage de l'Arinella, Lumio ❶ 04 95 60 78 47 ❶ 04 95 60 51 76 ❷ info@lematahari.com ❿ www.lematahari.com ❶ 12.00–16.00 Apr & May; 12.00–16.00 & 20.00–24.00 (closed Mon pm), June–Sept; closed Oct–Apr

A Flatta ££ In Calenzana, Chef Ludovic Quinton cooks up numerous Corsican specialities, and there are occasional themed evenings. ❶ 04 95 62 80 38 ❶ 04 95 62 86 30 ❷ contact@aflatta.com ❿ www.aflatta.com ❶ 12.00–14.00 & 19.30–20.00 Sat & Sun, 19.30–22.00 Mon–Fri

⬤ *Pigna is well known for its handicrafts*

Algajola

In between Calvi and l'Île Rousse, this small but elegant resort used to be a major port specialising in oysters and olive oil.
Ⓝ Take the N197 north from Calvi or south from l'Île Rousse

THINGS TO SEE & DO

There's a long sandy beach that stretches for about a mile right by the town. There are cafés and bars here, plus places from which to rent boats or windsurfing gear. The Citadel here is private property and not open for visits.

Produits Corses Costa
A shop housed in an old mill, full of traditional Corsican fare.
ⓣ 06 13 20 50 39 Ⓛ 09.00–12.00 & 14.00–19.00 Mon–Sat

AFTER DARK

Restaurants
Trois Guitares ££ This is the place to come for a traditional Corsican musical shindig. The owners make this place one of the most fun and interesting nights out on the island. ⓐ Route de l'Île Rousse ⓣ 04 95 60 11 05 Ⓛ 12.00–14.00 & 19.30–23.00

Saint-Florent

Saint-Florent is one of the island's most chic fishing villages. It's still fairly small, with a laid-back artistic feel, but has plenty of shops. It is a fairly short drive from Bastia – about 30 km (18 miles) away, right across the centre of the island, but at its narrowest point. The Old Town and the Citadel are full of lovely buildings painted dusky pinks and pale yellows. It's hard to believe that the Port de Plaisance was only built here in 1971: they've certainly made up for lost time since.

A bus service goes from Bastia to Saint-Florent year round (more frequent in summer ☎ 04 95 37 02 98) but no public transport around town

THINGS TO SEE & DO

The Plage de la Roya is the main beach – and not a bad one, at over 2 km (1¹/₄ miles) in length, and there's the small Plage d'Olzo which has big pudding stones, but is quieter. The real sun-worshippers head out to Agriates beaches, or get a *navette* (boat) round to Loto beach. In town, you're best to split your time between yacht-watching, sipping cappuccinos and poking around the Citadel and the windy streets that surround it. There are also the remains of the ramparts to explore – in fact, honestly, you'll find it hard to tear yourself away from Saint-Florent.

Citadelle
This is pretty hard to miss, as it looms right over the port. There's a circular tower that is a no-go area for tourists, but there is plenty more that you can see. There are lovely views back over the harbour.

◯ Saint-Florent turns to gold as the sun sets

Nebbio Cathedral (Église Santa Maria Assunta)

You need to walk 1 km (half a mile) up to this from the centre of Bastia, but it is one of the most important religious buildings in Corsica.

Place des Ports

This is the centre of most of the things that go on in Saint-Florent. It stands right between the Old Town and the swimming/sunbathing/boating areas – you can spend your time here either drinking coffee or watching the numerous *boules* players chancing their arm.

Plage de La Roya

OK, who's up for some pedalo action? It's just one of the many options here, from full-on scuba diving to the more genteel snorkelling.

Tip: Park your car at the big (paying) car park by the port and walk round – the whole place is easily navigable by foot, and it's just so pretty!

TAKING A BREAK

Restaurants

Ind'è Lucia ££ Traditional Corsican food, heartily enjoyed by the many regular visitors. ❷ Place Doria ❶ 04 95 37 04 15 ❶ 19.00–23.00, July–Oct

Restaurant Le Mathurin ££ A wine bar and restaurant converted from an old restaurant, where you get a good range of local wines and a tapas-style offering of local products. Great atmosphere. ❷ Old Town ❶ 04 95 37 04 48 ❶ 18.00–02.00 daily, May–Sept

---

❶ *Cafés line the streets in places such as Saint-Florent*

LIFESTYLE

Food & drink

Foodies are going to have fun here. Of course every area and village has its own specialities, and visitors to the region can have a great time getting to know what they like best.

CHARCUTERIE

Corsican charcuterie (*castagniccia*) is excellent – it is usually made by the producers rather than by butchers. The main products are *lonzu*, a kind of pork loin; the slightly stronger *coppa*; the Parma-ham-like *prizuttu* and the more thickly sliced *panzetta* (most like streaky bacon). One of the most sought-after pig-based products is *figatelli* (sausages made with smoked liver and other offal such as kidneys). Their season is from November to March, since that was when pigs were traditionally slaughtered, and they are eaten hot-dog style in a piece of bread. Look out for *figatelli*- and *prizuttu*-flavoured crisps in the supermarkets.

CHEESE

Locally made cheeses are either sheep or goats' milk, and most of it is made by the shepherds themselves – lots of the cheeses are known by the producer's name, rather than by type, making it a bit confusing to know what you're buying. *Brocciu* is the most famous Corsican cheese, a whey-based or *petit-lait* cheese produced from the autumn to the middle of summer. *Brocciu* is used as a basis for many dishes, both sweet and savoury – in its natural state it is a bit like cottage cheese, but tastier.

It tends to get flavoured with whatever is closest to hand. Expect to see it served fried into doughnuts (*beignets* in French, *fritelli* in Corsican) or eaten as it is, sprinkled with sugar and, for luxury, *eau de vie*. In fact, the latter is a popular and very tasty dessert – but approach with care, because you might not remember the rest of the evening.

Brocciu is also excellent used as a vegetable or pasta stuffing. Since 1998 there has been an AOC (Appellation d'Origine Contrôlée) for *brocciu*, which is a mark of quality regulation, and there are about 120 producers on the island. It doesn't really travel well, but anyone who wants to take some home can buy *brocciu passu*, which is salted and matured for several weeks.

Areas that are especially well known for it are Venacu (south of Corte), Calinzana (in the Balagne) and Bastelicaccia (near Ajaccio). These three types are soft and have washed skins. The cheeses of the Sartène areas (including Porto-Vecchio) are pressed and have dry crusts.

CHESTNUTS

Depending on where you are on the island, you'll find it hard to eat a meal without some type of chestnut in every course (and you might not even know it, because chestnut flour can be used to make bread or sauces, and even pastries).

Suppa di Castagne is the basis for a hearty soup that also has bones, onions, leeks, garlic and other flavourings. Chestnut desserts include doughnuts, tarts, cakes soaked in *eau de vie* – or, of course, mixed *brocciu* cheese. Look out also for *marrons glacés*; a local brand is known as *Dolci Corsi*.

FISH

In the Calvi region, the catch has diminished by half in 20 years, and the fishermen have to go to between 8 and 16 km (5 and 10 miles) out to find their fish and langoustes (and it's not just overfishing that depletes the stocks; the dolphins may look gorgeous to us, but they do eat a lot of fish! It is, however, still a thriving industry, and one that is highly picturesque, as most of the catch is sold on the quayside, bought directly by restaurants or sold in a few daily markets or by itinerant fishmongers. Check out types of fish in the menu decoder, on pages 98 and 99.

HONEY

The honey in Corsica is also amazing (not entirely surprising, given the amount of heather and flowers all over the island); it is the only one in France to have an appellation of its own, AOC Miel de Corse. The best villages for honey are Belgodère and Bastelica. This is quality stuff:

several beekeepers move their bees around to different sites in different seasons. Apparently maquis honey bees feast on 2,800 flower varieties, 127 of which are only found in Corsica. It is estimated that there are 17,000 beehives in Corsica.

Spring Honey – clear and delicate.
Maquis Honey – dark and strong.
Spring Maquis Honey – rich and caramelly.
Summer Maquis Honey – floral and fruity.
Autumn Maquis Honey – slightly bitter.
Chestnut Grove Honey – yes, chestnuts even make their way into the honey.

LOCAL WINE

The most well-known and widely made Corsican wine is also one of its simplest – and tastes lovely when accompanied by sunshine. It even sounds good: Vins de Pays de l'Île de Beauté.

Red, white and rosé wine is all produced on the island – with rosé being particularly well liked and accounting for about 30 per cent of production, not least because the island's closest mainland French wine is Provence, and they share many of the same grape varieties.

The quality of the wine in general has gone up enormously. You can still come across some horrors, but they are really trying to improve the standard, a fact that is demonstrated not least in the way that the majority of vines have been ripped up to concentrate on the best – in 2000 there were only 7,000 hectares (17,300 acres) of vines in Corsica compared to 32,000 hectares (79,070 acres) in 1976.

There are nine different appellations (wine regions) on the island: Patrimonio, Ajaccio, Muscat de Cap Corse, Vin de Corse, and five sub-areas within Vin de Corse (Coteaux de Cap Corse, Calvi, Sartène, Figari and Porto-Vecchio).

But what you really want to know is which ones to drink... The *vin de pays* is great, because it comes in all three colours, is light and refreshing and not too alcoholic. Also worth seeking out are the Muscats of Cap

🔺 *Traditional shops can still be found in Corsica*

Corse, sweet wines (called *vin doux naturel*), but not too sticky. Some of the island's best white wines also come from Cap Corse, such as Clos Nicrosi.

A useful site is Ⓦ www.vinsdecorse.com

A few good producers:

Clos Nicrosi
Lovely rich Muscats.
ⓐ 20047 Rogliano ☎ 04 95 35 41 17 🕐 Open by appointment only

Domaine Orsini
Shop and tasting room – wines and liqueurs.
ⓐ Calenzana, near Calvi ☎ 04 95 62 81 01 🖷 04 95 62 79 70
ⓔ info@domaine-orsini.com Ⓦ www.domaine-orsini.com 🕐 09.30–12.30 & 14.00–18.00

Comte de Peraldi
One of the most respected producers on the island.
ⓐ 20501 Ajaccio ☎ 04 95 22 37 30 🖷 04 95 20 92 91
ⓔ dom.peraldi@wanadoo.fr 🕐 Just drop in

Other Corsican alcohol
Cédratine is a liqueur made only in Corsica. One interesting product that has been developed by one of the island's producers, Mannarini, is *Liquore di Mele* made with honey.

The two Corsican aperitifs include Cap Corse (flavoured with quinine and slightly bittersweet, with a secret recipe of herbs).

Muscat grapes have a natural alcohol content of 15–16°, and most come from the micro-region of Cap Corse. Many wine makers also produce wines macerated in fruits, and so there is a *vin de clementine, vin d'orange, vin de cerise* and so on.

There are three beers – Pietra, an amber beer flavoured with chestnut; Serena, a light ale also flavoured with chestnut, and Colomba, a white, cloudy beer flavoured with herbs of the maquis. In July and

August you can visit the Pietra brewery 🕐 09.00–12.00 & 14.00–17.00 Mon–Fri (at other times of the year by appointment ☎ 04 95 30 14 70)

Apparently you can also get a Corsican whisky – newly created by the Pietra and Mavella distillery and named P&M after that. The malt is made in Pietra, using chestnut flour, and this is then transported south to Mavella to be distilled.

And the French national summer drink of Pastis has a new manufacturer in Corsica. Casanis is the oldest brand locally, but the new one is Mannarini from Corse Sud Distillerie.

And one non-alcoholic drink

You don't have to drink Coca Cola or Pepsi while you are on the island – there's Corsica Cola!

🔺 *An enticing food shop in Corte*

Menu decoder

Menus are typically in French. Smarter restaurants and restaurants in tourist resorts will probably have an English translation available.

Bar Sea bass

Brocciu cheese Fresh cheese made from ewe's whey; similar to ricotta

Canistrelli A traditional cake made with nuts, raisins or lemons that is often sprinkled with alcohol – usually pastis or wine

Cannelloni au brocciu Often on menus – tubes of pasta filled with local cheese, and usually a combination of herbs, chestnuts and meats

Castagniccia The world-renowned charcuterie that is native to Corsica! The main items that you will find on menus include: *Lonzu* (preserved pork loin served in paper-thin slices) *Coppa* (salted and peppered pork loin) *Figatelli* (small sausages made of finely chopped pigs' livers, kidneys or offal, served in wine and garlic, then smoked to get a wonderfully rich flavour)

Confit de canard/magret de canard All you really need to know is that these are two different cuts of duck, and are more complete pieces than you'll get with the lighter *salade de gesiers*. *Confit* is leg preserved in fat and *magret* is breast – and both will probably come served with thick-cut chips and a good mustard

Coquille Saint Jacques Scallop

Dorade Sea bream

Espadon Swordfish

Falculle Brioche, sweet bread – often dusted with tangy lemon, crusty sugar or *broccui* cheese

Fiadone Lemon tart – almost a cheesecake in consistency – made with the ubiquitous *brocciu* cheese, but flavoured with tart lemons

Frittella Doughnut

Friture Whitebait

Glace Ice cream – Corsica has the Italian influence here, and some really wonderful ice creams and sorbets, often made with real fruit, simply crushed up and frozen. Porto-Vecchio has some of the best on the island

Langoustes They are particularly big and juicy here, but fishing of them is banned between September and March to allow them to replenish their natural stocks. Even with that restriction in place, their numbers are dwindling

Lotte de mer Monkfish

Morue Cod

Oursins Sea urchins (often served raw or cooked into omelettes)

Porceddu Spit-roasted suckling pig, one of the island's most famous dishes. If you're (un)lucky, you might just see the whole thing being brought into the room, or roasted over a fire in front of you

Saint Pierre John Dory

Salade de chèvre chaud A regular on menus, this is a warm goat's-cheese salad that is usually served with chicory lettuce and a gorgeous sweet dressing of red onions and honey

Soupe Corse/Soupe Payanne The soup gets heartier as you move inland and uphill, but a version of this soup will be on most menus around the island. Expect a variation of a ham, olive oil, garlic, potatoes, pasta, vegetables and herbs – and yes, *brocciu* cheese makes the odd appearance in soup as well

Storzapreti *Brocciu* cheese dumplings, often served with mint or grilled into a gratin with grated cheese sprinkled on top

Stufatu Pasta and meat sauce

Shopping

Corsica is fiercely proud of its traditions, so expect lots of arts and crafts shops and galleries in both big cities and small villages. Goodies include hand-woven baskets, knives, wooden boxes, musical instruments and ceramics.

HANDICRAFTS

Shopping is mentioned in each of the resort write-ups above, with some suggestions of particularly good shops. The main thing to remember is that there are numerous markets, every day of the week, and many of the best things are to be found at these, rather than in shops (this is particularly true of foodstuffs). And because Corsica is still such an artisanal society in terms of producers, there are many workshops that it is possible to visit directly (such as Larna Corse near Corte – see page 85), rather than just visiting their shops in Ajaccio or Bastia.

Each area has its own specialities. For example, Balagne (just above Calvi) is where you'll find lots of traditional craft workshops. The village of Pigna specialises in making beautifully carved musical instruments.

CLOTHES & JEWELLERY

The towns, particularly the coastal resorts, have some very good clothes shops, from local boutiques to Parisian shops (often there's a nautical feel – but think millionaire yachts rather than fishing tugs...). Around the coast, inevitably things get more expensive.

There are some lovely jewellers, often specialising in simple silver pieces. Corsica's coral is very deep in colour and you're bound to come across some of it being sold as jewellery, but you should avoid buying it as the coral needs to be protected and buying such goods just encourages its destruction.

OILS & PERFUMES

Besides the chestnuts and honey on the breakfast table, the trees and flowers also translate into essential oils, and you'll find lots of these wherever you go. The oils are produced from flowers, leaves, seeds, bark, zest and wood, and include cedarwood, citronella, eucalyptus, fennel, juniper, lavender, mint, myrtle, thyme, verbena, wild carrot and many others. And one step up from essential oils, you can buy perfume made from violets, verbena and myrtle from Musée de la Perfumerie, Cynarom.

ⓐ 29 avenue Émile Sari, Bastia

WINE

Don't forget the wine. Besides buying bottles, look out for a tasting kit called Parfums de Corse. This has eight little smelling pots that give the typical aromas you get in Corsican wines (and on the island itself, so you can remember it after you've gone). Details from:

ⓦ www.vinsdecorse.com

⬤ *Typical Corsican woodcrafts for sale*

Children

As with much of mainland France, children are made very welcome. Throw in the Italian influence, and you have arms being opened wide to entertain your bambinos at every turn.

The island is well equipped and happy to receive younger visitors. For the youngest, there are plenty of beaches and aquariums; and for teenagers, there is surfing, mountain biking and wake-boarding – and scuba diving once they pass 16 years old (see page 105).

There's plenty to do as a family as well: young and old enjoy seeing dolphins and taking boat trips, and inland there are underground caves and crevices to explore, plenty of beautiful walking, plus some child-friendly petting zoos and donkey rides.

ADVENTURE
Tree-top climbing in the Gulf of Valinco (see page 69).

ANIMAL PARKS AND ZOOS
There are no full-scale wild-animal zoos in Corsica, but plenty of petting zoos and a large tortoise farm on the road between Ajaccio and Bastia.
Parc A Cupulatta ⓐ Route National 93, Vignola Vero, Vero ⓣ 04 95 52 82 34 ⓔ info@acupulatta.com ⓦ www.acupulatta.com

AQUARIUMS
Aquarium de Bonifacio Children will love the real caves that are found in this aquarium. ⓐ 71, Quai Comparetti, Bonifacio ⓣ and ⓕ 04 95 73 03 69

DONKEY RIDES
Donkey rides, Olmeto Plage (see page 69) and Sant'Antonino (see page 29).

It's also worth tracking down a good company that offers longer donkey treks around the Balagne region.
Balagn'ane ⓐ La Campanella, Olmi Cappella ⓣ 04 95 61 80 88 ⓔ info@rando-ane-corse.com ⓦ www.rando-ane-corse.com

HORSE RIDING

Horse-riding in Alta Rocca (see page 70) and Glacier de Brando
(see page 37).

Equiloisirs, near Corte, is very reliable, and has plenty of horses for
children. ⓐ Formation Animation Equitation, Pont de Papineschi, Corte
ⓣ 04 9561 09 88 ⓕ 04 95 61 09 88 ⓦ www.equiloisirs-fae.com
This website details horse-riding centres. ⓦ www.chevalencorse.com

TOURIST TRAINS

Almost all the coastal towns have tourist trains that take you around the
centre, or out to surrounding beaches. Just ask the tourist offices on
arrival – but here are two of the best:
Petit Train des Îles in Ajaccio (see page 20).
Le Petit Train, Bastia (see page 44).

WATER PARKS

Acqua Cyrne Gliss water park, Porticcio (see page 16).

⬤ Horses are popular all over the island

Sports & activities

If you like sports, either on the sea, river or mountains, you're going to be in heaven. Cycling is purely for the extremely enthusiastic, as we are talking seriously hilly terrain, but the views are amazing, and there are bike-hire places even in small villages. There is great horse-riding everywhere and, for more sedate days, thalassotherapy (seawater therapy).

BOATS

Corsica is heaven for all kinds of craft – small sailing boats, large motor boats, jet skis, tourist cruises... and everything in between.

Boat hire Algajola (see page 88); Ajaccio (see pages 20 & 65); and Bastia (see page 43).

Boat trips Bonifacio (see pages 55 & 74); Calvi (see page 29); and Porto (see page 79).

Canoeing Plage du Bussaglia, Porto (see page 23).

Kayaking As well as the Gulf of Galéria (see page 82), sea-kayaking is available in Barrettali, near Canari, Cap Corse (**Azimut** ❶ 04 95 38 25 25); in Bastelicaccia, near Ajaccio airport (**Cors'Aventure** ❸ Suaralta Vecchio ❶ 04 95 23 80 00); and in Calvi (**Calvi Nautique Club** ❸ Point Plage ❶ 04 95 35 96 84 ❸ cnc@calvinc.org ❿ www.calvinc.org ❶ July–Aug only).

FISHING

Most of the inland rivers are full of trout, salmon and eels that you can fish. A licence is needed first – contact Fédération Interdepartementale de Pêche en Corse ❸ Les Narcisse, Av Noel Franchini, 20090 Ajaccio ❶ 04 95 23 13 32

GOLF COURSES

Sperone, near Bonifacio, featuring 18 holes by Robert Trent Jones (see page 57). ❶ 04 95 73 17 13 ❿ www.sperone.com

Golf de Lezza, near Porto-Vecchio, which has 6 holes. ❶ 04 95 72 06 89 ❿ www.golf-delezza.com

Golf de Bastia at Borgo – 9 holes. ⓐ Route de l'aéroport, Castellarse
ⓣ 04 95 38 33 99

RAID INTER-LACS

The truly competitive can race around seven of the island's highest
inland lakes. Three hundred people maximum can join in. Contact:
ⓐ Rampe Saint Croix, 20250 Corte ⓣ 04 95 46 12 48
ⓦ www.interlacs.com

SKIING

The season tends to be January to March, sometimes going into April.
Best mountains are Ghisoni (1,580 m/5,183 ft), Col de Vergio (1,400 m/
4,593 ft), and Bastelica (1,600 m/5,249 ft).

SWIMMING

Swimming is possible both in the sea and in inland lakes and rivers.
There are flags that let you know if it's safe – green means no danger,
yellow means be careful (and that there is surveillance), red means
danger: swimming not allowed. Look out for sea snakes which, although
not too dangerous, are toxic and will sting, so be careful.

WATERSPORTS

There are opportunities to hire windsurfers and other watersports
equipment at many beaches, including Algajola (see page 88); Plage de
la Marana, Bastia (see page 43); Gulf of Valinco (see page 69); Plage de
Santa Giulia, Porto-Vecchio (see page 52); Olmeto Plage and Plage de
Santa Giulia, Propriano (see pages 60 & 61); and Plage de la Roya, Saint-
Florent (see page 90).

Scuba diving is a popular sport here, with centres in Calvi (see page
30); Cap Corse (see page 37); Gulf of Valinco (see page 69); l'Île Rousse
(see page 33); Propriano (see page 61); Saint-Florent (see page 90); and
Réserve Naturelle de Scandola (see page 81).

Festivals & events

A French island, with a heavily Italian influence and a largely Catholic population: is it any real surprise that there are a good number of festivals in Corsica?

The main festivals through the year are listed below, but this by no means covers everything. For other events, either check ahead with the local tourist offices, or just be pleasantly surprised while you're there.

January
Corbara et Agegno. The procession of Saint Antoine is held in various places all over the island.

February
Foirde de la Tubero (the first Sunday of February).

March
Fête de Notre-Dame de la Miséricorde, Ajaccio, 18 March. Our Lady is the patron saint of Ajaccio and this feast day is celebrated with a procession and fireworks.

Olive Oil Festival, Sainte-Lucie-de-Taliano. Every year in mid-March, the 'new olives' are given a royal welcome with a two-day festival where local producers get together and show off their products.

April
Saints' Week. This is the big one, with festivals, processions and special services all over Corsica. Some of the biggest include:

Procession du Christ Mort, Corte, where the roads and buildings are illuminated for a night procession on Maundy Thursday and Good Friday. There's a barefoot march for the truly penitent in **Calvi**, also on Good Friday.

And if you make it into **Sartène**, cars are banned from the Old Town for the night, and a procession takes place around the Church of Sainte-Marie. Starting at 21.30, the whole Old Town is lit with lanterns and candles.

May
Corsica Raid Adventure. Porticcio gets active with races in running, canyoning and kayaking. ☎ 04 95 25 16 16 Ⓦ www.corsicaraid.com

June
Cyclocorsica. All over the island, you're encouraged to get on your bike and ride. ☎ 04 95 21 96 94
Fête de Saint Jean Baptiste. Now it's the turn of Bastia's patron saint: celebrations are held over the midsummer weekend.
Calvi Jazz Festival. Held during the third week of June, several big-name international musicians play at this festival every year, and in the evenings from 23.00, there are jam sessions along by the port. Many of the concerts are free. ⓐ Office Municipal de Tourisme de Calvi ☎ 04 95 65 23 57/04 95 65 16 67 ⓔ info@calvi-jazz-festival.com Ⓦ www.calvi-jazz-festival.com

July
Foire du Vin, Luri. The island's biggest wine festival. ☎ 04 95 35 06 44 Ⓦ www.acunfraternita.com
Grand Raid Inter-lacs, Corte. Make the most of the inland lakes with fun sporting events around the highest lakes on the island – there are walks and races for different levels. Ⓦ www.interlacs.com
Estivoce (Summer Voice), **Pigna and La Balagne**. Lasting ten days in early July, singers and musicians group together for one of the best musical events on the island. ☎ 04 95 61 73 13 Ⓦ www.festivoce.casa-musicale.org

August
Roman Festival, Aleria. For two days in early August, the village of Aleria comes over all Ancient Rome, with open-air markets, mini-Olympiads, costumed evenings and Roman wine tasting.
Jazz and Guitar Festival, Erbalunga, second week of August. ☎ 04 95 33 20 84

September
Santa di u Niolu, Casamaccioli. One of the island's most important religious festivals takes place over three days in early September.

October
Tour de la Corse Automobile. Classic cars are driven all over the island from the second week of October, leaving from Ajaccio ☏ 04 95 23 62 60
La Festival du Vent (the Wind Festival) in Calvi features kite flying, windsurfing and plenty of live music.
ⓦ www.lefestivalduvent.com

November
Arte-Mare, Bastia. Each year organised around a different theme, and with a different partner city, the festival takes as its inspiration the Mediterranean and its many treasures.

December
A fiera di a Castagna, Bocognano. Corsica's biggest regional shindig, with chestnut producers gathering around to show you just exactly what can be done with this unassuming foodstuff. ☏ 04 95 27 41 76
ⓦ www.fieradiacastagna.com

 Signposts on typically hilly terrain

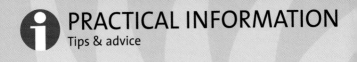

Preparing to go

GETTING THERE

By sea

Being an island, the easiest (and certainly most picturesque) way to reach Corsica is by sea. Routes between France and Corsica, Italy and Corsica, and Sardinia and Corsica are covered by traditional ferries or high-speed hovercraft. From France, you can sail from Marseille, Nice and Toulon all year to Ajaccio and Bastia. Marseille also has year-round boats to Calvi, l'Île Rousse, Porto-Vecchio and Propriano. The main ports from Italy are Genoa and Naples.

Obviously journey times vary, depending on whether you take slow or fast boats (and on the weather) but generally speaking it will take around three to four hours between Nice and Bastia, or five and six between Nice and Ajaccio. There are also overnight ferries that take around 12 hours and arrive in time for breakfast. There might be three or four sailings a day over summer, but only one a day over winter – always check ahead with the various companies.

Corsica Ferries

ⓐ 5 bis, rue Chanoine Leschi, 20296 Bastia ⓣ 04 95 32 95 95/08 25 09 50 95 ⓕ 04 95 32 40 07 ⓔ agency@corsicaferries.com ⓦ www.corsicaferries.com

La Méridionale (CMN)

ⓣ 04 95 76 04 36 ⓦ www.cmn.fr
The main company sailing between Marseille and Corsica, it also has a number of services to Sardinia from Corsica.

MobyLines

ⓣ 04 95 34 84 94 ⓦ www.mobylines.com
Best for trips to and from Italian ports.

SNCM

ⓣ 08 25 88 80 88 ⓦ www.sncm.fr
This was the first company to introduce high-speed hovercraft, bringing the time down to just over three hours from Nice to Ajaccio, compared to six hours on a normal car ferry.

By air

It's not as easy to fly to Corsica as you might imagine for such an ideal holiday destination – and cheap flights are even harder to find. The major airlines serve the island well, though, particularly Air France.

If you're leaving from France, direct flights fly to all four of Corsica's airports from most major cities, including Paris, Lyon, Bordeaux, Nantes, Strasbourg, Toulouse, Marseille, Toulon and Nice (direct in high season, almost always with a stop in Paris at other times of the year). Flights are also available from other European cities, including London, and from most UK airports, but often with a change in Paris or London.

British Airways (and **GB Airways**, who are now operating as British Airways) fly from Gatwick to Bastia and Ajaccio. ☎ 0870 8509 850 Ⓦ www.ba.com

Air France (and **CCM Airlines**, who are a partner of Air France but are now operating as one company) fly from most mainland destinations – often with a connection in Paris – to Figari, Bastia and Ajaccio. ☎ 0870 142 4343 Ⓦ www.airfrance.com

KLM and **Lufthansa** also fly there, but with changes to partner airlines. And of course it's always worth trying aggregate sites such as Ⓦ www.corse-moins-cher.com, Ⓦ www.opodo.com, www.lastminute.com and www.expedia.com

Many people are aware that air travel emits CO_2, which contributes to climate change. You may be interested in the possibility of lessening the environmental impact of your flight through the charity Climate Care, which offsets your CO_2 by funding environmental projects around the world. Visit Ⓦ www.climatecare.org

Package holidays

Package holiday and charter flight specialists to Corsica include:

Travelgate Ltd, a very useful company that offers a wide variety of offers from different companies, including many last-minute package deals. Having identified the one you want, you usually contact the relevant company directly.

Ⓐ 7 King Edward's Grove, Teddington, Middlesex TW11 9LY, UK ☎ 020 8287 5527 Ⓦ www.travelgate.co.uk

Voyages Ilena

Corsica and Sardinia specialists

📍 1 Old Garden House, The Lanterns, Bridge Lane, London SW11 3AD

📞 020 7924 4440 📠 020 7924 4441 🌐 www.voyagesilena.co.uk

Corsican Places

📍 Cutter House, 1560 Parkway, Solent Business Park, Fareham, Hampshire PO15 7AG, UK 🌐 www.corsica.co.uk

TRAVEL INSURANCE

Visitors from the UK are covered by EU reciprocal health schemes while in France. You should take a European Health Insurance Card (EHIC) with you when you go; this can be obtained free of charge through most UK post offices or through the UK Department of Health via their website (🌐 www.dh.gov.uk) or by telephoning 📞 0845 6062030 (from outside the UK call (0044) 191203555).

The EHIC is not a substitute for medical and travel insurance, but entitles you to emergency medical treatment on the same terms as French nationals. You will not be covered for medical repatriation, on-going medical treatment or treatment of a non-urgent nature. Always make sure you have adequate travel insurance, covering not only health, but possessions, etc. All non-EU travellers should also make sure they have adequate insurance before they travel.

You also need to think about taking out specialist insurance if you are planning on scuba diving or doing any other adventure sports during your Corsican holiday.

It's also worth knowing that, as with any tourist resort, there are frequent reports of pickpocketing from bars at night – and it is not advised to leave valuables in your car while you head off to the beach.

TOURISM AUTHORITY

There is a new number within France to ring and get any tourist board you want. Just call 3264 (it costs €0.34/minute), and state clearly the place that you want. You will be put through automatically.

There are two 'umbrella' organisations for tourism to Corsica:

Agence du Tourisme de la Corse
17 boulevard Roi-Jerome, BP 19, 20181 Ajaccio cedex 01
📞 04 95 51 00 00 📞 04 95 51 14 40 ✉️ info@visit-corsica.com
🌐 www.visit-corsica.com

Maison de la France (French Tourist Board)
They have a UK branch that can offer plenty of info before you leave: 🏠 178 Piccadilly, London W1J 9AL 📞 09068 244 123 (60p/minute at all times) 📞 020 7493 6594 ✉️ info.uk@franceguide.com 🌐 http://uk.franceguide.com

BEFORE YOU LEAVE

You don't need any vaccinations to visit France, nor do you need to take any particular precautions, although if you are taking prescription medication it is wise to take your own supply with you. Other than that, it's a good idea to pack a few obvious items such as a travelling first-aid kit, a hat and sunblock. But all important items will be available to buy locally in any Corsican holiday resort.

ENTRY FORMALITIES

Citizens of EU countries, the USA, Canada, Australia, New Zealand and Ireland who hold valid passports do not need a visa to visit for less than 90 days. If you want to stay for longer than three months, you need to put in a request at the Prefecture of Ajaccio (🏠 Palais Lantivy, Cours Napoléon, 20188 Ajaccio 📞 04 95 11 12 13 📞 04 95 11 10 28, 🌐 www.corse.pref.gouv.fr). For all entries, you need an identity card with photograph, which means a passport. South African passport holders must also have a Schengen visa.

For drivers, an international driving licence is required, together with a valid insurance certificate. And don't forget if you're hiring a car to take your paper certificate as well as your smaller card with the photo ID.

MONEY

Corsica uses euros, just as they do in mainland France. Notes are available in five, 10, 20, 50, 100 and 500 euro denominations, with one and two euro coins, and the smaller change (below one euro) in cents. For current exchange rates, check www.travelex.com or www.oanda.com

Credit cards are widely accepted in hotels, restaurants and bars in all the major towns, but it is very wise to keep cash with you in some of the more remote areas. The general rule is, the further inland you go, the more you will be reliant upon cash. Traveller's cheques are accepted in the major cities, but are likely to be looked at with a blank expression in the more remote areas.

CLIMATE

The climate is usually warm and gentle year-round, as Corsica is located in the Gulf of Genes. Corsica is sunnier than anywhere in mainland France, and gets 2,900 hours of sunshine per year. However, if you're up in the mountains, you'll need a sweater because it will get cold at night, even in the summer months.

Generally, winters are clear and mild – temperatures stay around 18°C (64°F). In the ski resorts (Bastelica, Ghisoni, Cuscione), there is almost always good snow from January to April, but check ahead. From March, things heat up and temperatures should reach an average of 25°C (75°F) by June – but it will still feel like winter if you venture into the sea. In high summer temperatures can easily reach 36°C (97°F), especially along the coast (they might be up to 10°C/20°F lower inland). Autumns deliver lovely, warm, sunny days, and the sea hasn't cooled down too much yet, so the really brave can still go swimming.

BAGGAGE ALLOWANCE

Always check with your airline, as allowances change frequently at the moment. During normal conditions, most airlines allow 20 kg (44 lb) of luggage per person (excluding infants). This will be confirmed to you either at the time of booking or when your tickets are sent out. If you wish to check in any bulky items (such as skis or surfboards, for example), always inform your airline ahead of arriving at the airport.

⬤ *Now, where did I leave my towel?*

During your stay

AIRPORTS

There are four airports on the island:

Aeroporto d'Ajaccio (Campo dell'Oro)
🕾 04 95 23 56 56 🕸 www.ajaccio.aeroport.fr
Not surprisingly, the capital city has the biggest airport on the island, and has the most flights.

Aeroporto de Bastia (Poretta)
🅐 Lucciano (25 km/15 miles south of Bastia) 🕾 04 95 54 54 54
🕸 www.calvi.aeroport.fr

Aeroporto de Calvi (Sta Catarina)
🕾 04 95 65 88 88 🕸 www.calvi.aeroport.fr

Aeroporto de Figari-Sud Corse
🕾 04 95 71 10 10 🕸 www.figari.aeroport.fr
This airport is near Bonifacio, and so is the best one for visiting southern Corsica and Sardinia.

COMMUNICATIONS
Phones

There is good mobile phone coverage in all the main towns, but things can get a little less reliable as soon as you head into the interior of the island. And when you do have coverage, don't forget that when using a British mobile phone, you need to dial 00 33 and then drop the first 0 of the Corsican phone number.

Most public payphones now take credit cards, or you can buy telephone cards from any *tabac*. Simply pick up the receiver, and wait for the screen to change from either '*Decrochez*' or '*Patientez s'il vous plaît*' to '*Introduire carte ou faire numero libre*' – this means insert your card or dial a toll-free number.

Postal services

For those wanting to send postcards back home, there is a good network of post offices in even the smallest villages, and postal times back to mainland France or to the UK are reasonable. Stamps cost 54 cents (€0.54) for postage within France, and 60 cents (€0.60 euros) for the UK and the rest of the European Union. Postage to outside of the EU is 85 cents (€0.85).

Internet access

All the major hotels have internet access, and increasingly have WiFi access within rooms, although there will be a surcharge for this, usually €5 per day.

Elsewhere, ADSL high-speed access is already available in big centres – and even in some mountain villages – and you'll find internet cafés in all the tourist centres. The rate of connection via ADSL in Corsica is at 10.5 per cent (versus the national level of 8.5 per cent in mainland France), but to achieve high-speed internet connection everywhere will be quite a challenge, given the mountainous terrain over much of the island. There is also a project called 'Corsica Hotspot', which is currently establishing 40 free internet access hotspots in town halls, stations, libraries, cafés, airports and so on. It is hoped that this will be extended across the island by 2008.

TELEPHONE CODES

To dial Corsica from abroad, dial the international access code (00), followed by the country code, 33. Then omit the first 0 of the area code.

When dialling abroad from Corsica, the following codes are required (and you then need to drop the first 'o' of the number)

England +44   **US** + 1   **Australia** +61   **Ireland** + 353
New Zealand + 64   **South Africa** + 27

Language

When consulting maps and reading directions that you've been given, watch out for spellings – some places use the Italian and some the French version.

CUSTOMS

Corsicans are fiercely proud of their heritage, and you will be made to feel very welcome, particularly if you just spend a few minutes praising the beauty of the island.

In terms of customs, Corsicans retain many of their traditional ways of life – you can tell this very easily, simply by wandering into a craft shop and seeing the vast array of traditionally made products (see Shopping section). It's still very much an artisan society – cheeses are made by the shepherd who looks after the goats and sheep, dried meats are made by the same farmer that tends the herds, chestnut jams are made by the growers who tend the chestnut trees.

As with any culture, the language gives a big clue to the customs and heritage of the island. The Corsican language is heavily influenced by its Italian ancestry, although is still recognisably French, and is spoken with a heavy local dialect (often the ends of words are swallowed, so they might say Porto-Vec rather than Porto-Vecchio). 'Mainland' French will of course also be spoken and understood everywhere, and the written language is far more recognisably French.

EMERGENCY PHRASES

Help! Au secours! *Ossercoor!*   **Fire!** Au feu! *Oh fur!*
Stop! Stop! *Stop!*
Call an ambulance/a doctor/the police/the fire service!
Appelez une ambulance/un médecin/la police/les pompiers!
Ahperleh ewn ahngbewlahngss/ang medesang/lah poleess/leh pompeeyeh!

But even if you can speak French, you're never going to forget that this isn't mainland France. You'll see the 'other' national flag pretty much everywhere. It's known as the Moor's head flag and dates back to the late 18th century when Pascal Paoli (the father of the Corsican freedom movement, dubbed 'Corsica's George Washington') made a few alterations to a previous flag which had a blindfolded Moor in chains, and gave this one his official blessing.

DRESS CODES

There are a number of hotels and restaurants that prefer men to wear long trousers to dinner, but Corsica does have Italian as well as French heritage, and there is no need to worry about being too formal. Just ensure, as with all Catholic countries, that you cover up well when going into churches. Topless sunbathing is also frowned upon in almost all of the resorts.

ELECTRICITY

As in mainland France, the Corsicans use two-pin plugs at 220 volts. Visitors from the UK will need an adaptor.

EMERGENCIES

The main hospitals are in Ajaccio and Bastia. To speed up practicalities before treatment, ensure you have your EHIC card (available from Ⓦ www..ehic.org.uk ❶ 0845 606 2030 or from some post offices) before you leave the UK.

EMERGENCY NUMBERS

SAMU (ambulance emergency services): 15
Urgence (police): 17
The Commissariat de Police in Ajaccio: ❶ 04 95 11 17 17
Les Pompiers (fire): 18

Centre Hospitalier Départemental de Castelluccio

ⓐ Rte St Antoine, Ajaccio ⓣ 04 95 29 36 36 ⓕ 04 95 29 37 63

Centre Hospitalier General

ⓐ Rte Imperiale Paese Nouvo, Bastia ⓣ 04 95 59 11 11

GETTING AROUND

Car hire

When hiring a car you will be asked to show your passport and an EU or international driving licence. The major care hire companies have offices at the airports and in the cities and resorts. You can usually get the best deal by reserving a car from home at the same time as making a flight or holiday booking.

Avis ⓣ 0 820 05 05 05 ⓦ www.avis.fr

Hertz ⓣ 01 39 38 38 38 ⓦ www.hertz.fr

DRIVING RULES & CONDITIONS

Driving in Corsica can be hair-raising at times (in fact, pretty much all the time), so be careful and drive slowly on winding roads – and make use of your horn.

Don't be fooled by the fact that this is a holiday island: the same rules of the road apply here as in mainland France. This means that there are speed cameras in most of the major cities, and police checkpoints for speeding at regular intervals, especially in summer.

Remember to fill up your petrol tank regularly as, once you are out of town, petrol stations can be few and far between.

Speed limits are:

50 km/h (30 mph) in towns and built-up areas

90 km/h (56 mph) on *routes nationales* (main roads)

130km/h (80 mph) on motorways; 110 km/h (68 mph) when wet

Sardinia: the speed limit on motorways is 120km/h (75 mph).

Bus

If you're planning on using buses, resign yourself to the fact that you'll pretty much have to stick to the main towns. Services are fairly frequent between Bastia, Corte and Ajaccio, and along the east coast from Bastia to Porto-Vecchio and Bonifacio, and Ajaccio and Bastia particularly have a good network of smaller local buses that run between the main attractions and to some of the surrounding beaches. However, some of the most scenic stretches of the west coast (between Porto and Calvi, for example), and large chunks of the interior, are off limits for much of the year without your own vehicle.

Local bus routes are detailed in each section, but the best way to check up-to-date local bus information is to call a tourist office, or use the slightly scrappy website ⓦ www.corsicabus.org

Train

If you decide to stay off the roads, you can do worse than take the local trains.

They might be a bit slow and unreliable, but they do offer some of the best views of the island, and are excellent value. They also link all the major centres on the island, although you're going to find it difficult to get the train to the more remote towns on the island.

This is an island that is made for taking the train, and it's packed with tourist train routes, from cute, open-air little rides around town, to longer, more scenic routes through the mountains and along the coast. One of the best is 'U Trinichellu' (meaning little train but commonly nicknamed 'the trembler') from Ajaccio to Vizzavona, several thousand metres up in the centre of the island. Info on this from Ajaccio train station ⓘ 04 95 23 11 03 or ⓦ www.ter.sncf.com/trains-touristiques/corse.htm

You can also buy a 'Zoom' card that gives unlimited train travel around Corsica for one week for just €47.

HEALTH, SAFETY & CRIME

Health

No inoculations are necessary for British citizens travelling to Corsica. If you have any queries, it is always worth talking to your doctor before leaving, or reading the Department of Health leaflet T5 'Health Advice for Travellers', available at most UK post offices, or visiting Ⓦ www.dh.gov.uk (section Travel Advice). It's always advisable to take a small first-aid kit with you and keep it in the car if you are travelling around.

If you take regular medication, take enough for your holiday. You should consider taking your regular headache or seasickness remedy with you as well. There are plenty of pharmacies on Corsica, however, in which to buy sun tan lotion and other beach necessities, but prices can be a bit high in the tourist areas such as Porto-Vecchio.

Safety & crime

There is very little violent crime on Corsica, and the most common form of crime is pickpocketing.

However, there have been some well-publicised incidents recently of Corsican separatists targeting French second-home-owners on the island. Although these incidents get a lot of press, they are far from frequent, and you shouldn't really have any problems while on the island (although we wouldn't recommend draping yourself in the Tricolour and singing *La Marseillaise* on every street corner).

MEDIA

The main Corsican paper is the *Corse Matin*, but you can also easily get the mainland French papers of *Le Figaro* and *Le Monde*. A good local 'lifestyle' magazine is *Terra Corsa*.

OPENING HOURS

These do vary a bit, depending on whether you are in 'Italian' resorts like Porto-Vecchio, where things tend to open and close later, or in more French resorts like Bastia, which follow the mainland opening hours.

But generally speaking, opening hours are as follows:

Banks 🕐 08.30–14.45 Mon–Fri

Shops 🕐 09.30/10.00–12.30 & 02.30–19.00 Mon–Sat

Pharmacies 🕐 08.30/09.00–12.00 & 14.00-19.00 Mon–Sat

Restaurants 🕐 12.00–14.00, 19.00–22.30 Mon–Sun (although some restaurants are closed Mon)

In Sardinia, or mainland Italy, opening hours tend to be:

Banks 🕐 08.30–13.30 & 14.30–16.00 Mon–Fri

Shops 🕐 09.30-13.30 & 16.30–20.00 Mon–Sat

Pharmacies 🕐 09.30–13.30 & 16.00–20.00 Mon–Sat

RELIGION

Corsica has a largely Roman Catholic population, still with a strong churchgoing tradition. This also means there are many religious festivals and religious public holidays – one of the largest being over Easter, with numerous processions being held during Saints' Week.

Just about everything is closed on Sundays (although some supermarkets may stay open on Sunday morning).

TIME DIFFERENCES

Corsica is in the same time zone as mainland Europe, which means it is one hour ahead of the UK.

TIPPING

A 15 per cent service charge is included in the bill in restaurants, although often not in cafés, so check in advance. Even with this included, it is often customary to add another 2–3 per cent on top if the service has been good (at the very least, it's always appropriate to round the bill up to the nearest euro), but remember that French waiters don't live for tips alone – they do have the health care and pension benefits that all French employees have. Taxi drivers expect 10 per cent of the fare on top; hairdressers too would expect about 10 per cent. When staying in hotels, staff will expect a tip of several euros for carrying baggage to rooms.

TOILETS

Generally speaking these are now British-style, although you still might be unlucky and get a few 'hole-in-the-ground' types so loved in France until the 1980s.

TRAVELLERS WITH DISABILITIES

There are a few beaches with good disabled access (which tends only to mean they have a simple strip of good grip floor carpet covering a strip of sand, allowing wheels to roll along the beach easily):

La Plage de la Viva, Porticcio (near Ajaccio)
La Plage de l'Arinella, Bastia
La Plage aux Boucaniers, La Marana

There are also two useful contacts for finding the best restaurants, bars, museums etc for wheelchair and disabled access:
ⓐ 159 bis, rue Dr Del Pelligrino, Ajaccio ⓣ 04 95 20 75 33

Immeuble San Petru ⓐ Bâtiment à Route Impériale Ajaccio
ⓣ 04 95 30 86 01 ⓦ www.apf.asso.fr

ACKNOWLEDGEMENTS

The publishers would like to thank the following individuals and organisations for providing their copyright photographs for this book:

World Pictures pages 39, 53, 72, 76; all the rest, Jacqueline Fryd.

Copy editor: Penny Isaac
Proofreader: Ian Faulkner

Send your thoughts to
books@thomascook.com

- Found a beach bar, peaceful stretch of sand or must-see sight that we don't feature?

- Like to tip us off about any information that needs a little updating?

- Want to tell us what you love about this handy, little guidebook and more importantly how we can make it even handier?

Then here's your chance to tell all! Send us ideas, discoveries and recommendations today and then look out for your valuable input in the next edition of this title. And, as an extra 'thank you' from Thomas Cook Publishing, you'll be automatically entered into our exciting prize draw.

Send an email to the above address or write to:
HotSpots Project Editor, Thomas Cook Publishing, PO Box 227, Unit 18, Coningsby Road, Peterborough PE3 8SB, UK